Women Mean Business

Women Mean Business

Successful Strategies for Starting Your Own Business

Moneca Litton

KEY PORTER BOOKS

Canadian Cataloguing in Publication Data

Litton, Moneca, 1944 –
Women mean business

Bibliography: p.
Includes index.
ISBN 1-55013-017-X

1. New Business enterprises. 2. Women in business. I. Title.

HD62.5.L58 1987 658.1'1'024042 C87-093334-5

Key Porter Books Limited
70 The Esplanade
Toronto, Ontario
Canada M5E 1R2

Design: Marie Bartholomew
Typesetting: Robinson Communications Group
Printed and bound in Canada by Webcom Ltd.

87 88 89 90 6 5 4 3 2 1

CONTENTS

DEDICATED TO WOMEN ENTREPRENEURS,
THOSE WITH INTENT TO BE,
AND THOSE STILL DREAMING.

ACKNOWLEDGEMENTS

The author gratefully acknowledges the expertise and support of all women interviewed, whether mentioned in the book or not, as well as that of Brian Hann, Manager of Independent Business of The Royal Bank of Canada in Vancouver. Also my agent, who tried to ignore me but couldn't, my editor, whom I tried to ignore but couldn't, and my publisher, who was insightful enough to make the book possible. I wish to acknowledge, too, my friends, especially Don M.E. Hamilton, who were instrumental in helping me maintain my vision. Thank you, Altadea.

For permission to reprint or adapt their work, I am indebted to the following authors, publishers and organizations: Many entries in the Glossary (pages 183 to 187) are based on David Crane, *A Dictionary of Canadian Economics* (Edmonton: Hurtig, 1980). They are reprinted by permission of the publisher. The list of organizations (pages 175 to 181) is reprinted by permission of *The Globe and Mail,* Toronto. Sources include government and private agencies, Ernst and Whinney, and Sources of Funds Index. The checklist (pages 146 to 147) is from *The Entrepreneur's Complete Self-Assessment Guide* by Douglas A. Gray, International Self-Counsel Press Ltd., 1986. Reprinted courtesy of the publisher. The start-up quiz (pages 16 to 17), business plan (pages 72 to 74), marketing strategy (pages 100 to 101) and classification (pages 126 to 127) are reprinted or adapted from William Jennings, *Entrepreneurship: A Primer for Canadians,* (Toronto, 1985). Reprinted courtesy of the Canadian Foundation for Economic Education. The quotation (page 1) is from Madonna Kolbenschlag, *Kiss Sleeping Beauty Good-Bye,* (New York: Doubleday & Company Inc., 1979). The "notorious characters" (page 143) are reprinted with permission from *How to Get Control of Your Time and Your Life,* copyright © 1973 by Alan Lakein. Published by

David McKay Company, Inc. Reprinted by permission of the publisher. The franchise industry growth chart (page 153) is from *The Future of Franchising* by The Naisbitt Group, published by the International Franchise Association, Washington, D.C. The analysis of partnerships (page 145) is reprinted from *The Self-Employed Woman,* copyright © 1985 by Jeanette Reddish Scollard. Reprinted by permission of Simon & Schuster, Inc. The personal history exercise (page 18) is adapted from Sandra Winston, *The Entrepreneurial Woman,* (New York: Newsweek Books, 1979). Copyright © 1979 by Newsweek Inc. Reprinted by permission of the publisher.

Care has been taken to trace ownership of copyright material contained in this book. The author will gladly receive any information that will enable her to rectify errors or omissions affecting references or credit lines in subsequent editions.

INTRODUCTION

You see them in high school study halls, twisting their tresses and staring out the window. You see them in offices filing stacks of reports and glancing at the clock anxiously. You see them in laundromats, in supermarkets, in beauty parlours, on buses. You see them on the couch, TV blaring, paging through *Seventeen* magazine. Wherever you see them, they are young, anxious, languid, bored, unsatisfied with themselves. . . . They all have one thing in common: They are convinced they are waiting for something. They imagine themselves in a state of readiness, of expectancy, of waiting for life and for their real existence to begin. In fact, it has already begun — it is passing them by. . . . They are sleeping beauties who may never wake up.

Madonna Kolbenschlag
Kiss Sleeping Beauty Good-Bye

According to the Canadian Federation of Independent Business, of the 75,000 new businesses started in 1984, two-thirds were started by women. It would seem that vast numbers of Canadian sleeping beauties are no longer content to wait for Prince Charming. What they are discovering is that the maiden is awake and in business for herself.

In a 1981 study of women and men entrepreneurs conducted by management consultants Laventhol & Horwath entitled "The Rise of Female Capitalism — Women as Entrepreneurs," it was determined that "women are a major force in small business, are more successful than men, and are responsible for a significant portion of job creation in Canada." The business survival rate of women entrepreneurs is 47 per cent, in comparison with men at 25 per cent, at the end of the three-year start-up stage. If trends continue (and there is no reason to believe they will not), no one needs a crystal ball to foretell who will be holding the majority of power and money by the turn of the century.

The reasons why women choose self-employment appear simple enough: financial independence, control over their lives, the challenge, and the desire to be their own boss. But what they may be choosing, in fact, is power. Claude Bruneau and Barbara Allen writing in *Business Quarterly* explore the theory "that by expressing such a strong interest in money, women may be reclaiming the power that they enjoyed in other societies and lost." Anthropologists such as Marjorie Shostak claim women in nomadic societies played key roles as income providers. They were highly regarded in the workforce, since the tasks they performed were necessary for survival. When the cooperative system of the nomadic societies was replaced with an agricultural one, it diminished women's economic role as well as their status. And it was only a matter of time before the women who worked alongside their husbands in the fields (and kept the books, as well) would be pushed aside in favour of men and machines and the Industrial Revolution. With this revolution came a patriarchal society that would not value women as economic contributors, and would relegate them to their homes. A reclaiming of power has taken place slowly throughout this century and particularly during the last ten years, as more women attain management positions as well as create their own power through entrepreneurship.

Who are these women who are shaking up the old boys' stronghold? First of all, there is nothing exclusive about successful women entrepreneurs. There is no age, colour, nationality, religion, education, region, or social standing that defines the majority of them. There is only one common denominator — the burning desire to succeed. Among such women are the secretary who was fired when she was no longer content to be an extension of the wife who serves at home; the bank teller who could not climb higher than a loans officer; the wife whose husband became unemployed, and the business grad who realized that her only chance for a key to the executive washroom was to own the company. While research on entrepreneurship is limited in general, and scant on female entrepreneurs specifically, sociologists and economists now share the task of interpreting this phenomenon of the eighties.

In a 1985 study I conducted for The Royal Bank of Canada on "The Relationship of Female Entrepreneurship with Lending Institutions in Western Canada," the respondents (like those in other surveys across the country) openly shared their entrepreneurial experience in the hope of shedding light on some sister's dream. The study determined that women start businesses for many reasons: for the challenge, the desire to be their own boss, the chance for financial independence, the desire to implement a great idea, the freedom to choose their own hours, the need to get away from a dead-end job. or the desire to be at home with their children while earning money.

Women Mean Business was possible in part due to this study. It was also made possible because of my lecturing to thousands of women on the subject of entrepreneurship and getting their feedback. Personal, written, and phone interviews also form an integral part of this book. The ideas gleaned from books and periodicals have been credited throughout the text. Where no reference to a print source is indicated, the information or quotation is taken from those interviews.

The book is not intended to be the final word on any particular chapter or area of expertise. It was written as a basic strategy for the implementation of dreams. Its publication fulfills one of mine.

Moneca Litton

Chapter 1

SO YOU WANT TO BE AN ENTREPRENEUR

Don't be the person with the great ideas who watches everyone else steal them and open *your* business.

Tera Hallgren,
Partner, Cookies by George

This book is designed to help you launch your own idea — and keep it. The decision to create a venture is a personal one. It involves in part the need for self-confidence, the ability to take risks, and a dogged determination. Whether you work from your home or set up shop elsewhere, starting a business can turn out to be your greatest disappointment or the thrill of a lifetime. Either way, most new entrepreneurs find the experience an emotional and financial roller coaster. This is your opportunity to assess your personal as well as business skills *before* you quit your job, mortgage your home, rent your storefront, or buy your computer on time.

Entrepreneurship — what is it, who wants it, and how do they get it? *The Concise Oxford Dictionary* has it about right: "*Entrepreneur* (n.), person in effective control of commercial undertaking; one who undertakes a business or enterprise, with chance of profit or loss." That chance for profit or loss is the challenge shared by all entrepreneurs, and what influences that chance is your knowledge of yourself and your business skills.

In a 1986 article in the Toronto *Globe and Mail,* U.S. management guru Peter Drucker claims that entrepreneurship can be learned, and Executive Director Keith McPherson of the Entrepreneurship Institute of Canada says that it can't. It seems that somewhere in the middle may lie a formula for developing entrepreneurial skills through encouragement, strong guidance, and reference to successful examples. Both men seem to agree that "by nature entrepreneurs are restless, good leaders, can work under pressure, and think the world of themselves and their ideas."

Being the boss for many women represents the fastest track into the economic mainstream. Lance Secretan, author of *Managerial Moxie,* says, "Because women are still so extensively discriminated against in business, there is only one female CEO in the Fortune 500 group of the largest industrial companies in the United States." In Canada, according to a Conference Board of Canada survey, women hold only 2.5 per cent of corporate directorships.

This situation is soon to be rectified by entrepreneurs like Meg Mitchell, president of the executive recruitment firm The Thomas-Mitchell Association Inc. "In 1982," reports Mitchell, "when everyone in the executive search field was so depressed about how bad business was, I decided it was a good time for a fresh approach, and aimed for a niche no one was in. Now, with the recovery well under way, companies are again actively looking for women board members.'' The company takes a new tack by providing a talent-bank of well-qualified women for corporate consideration. Coming from a family that encouraged entrepreneurship, and armed with eight years of experience and four years of savings, Mitchell was ready when opportunity knocked.

More and more women are listening to that knock of opportunity. According to Dina Lavoie, quoted in the Montreal *Gazette,* female entrepreneurs have ''more training, more encouragement, more sectors, more numbers and more dollars than ever before.'' Lavoie says that women who start businesses fall into three basic categories:

The Sponsored Entrepreneur — She is usually between 40 and 44. She is helped along and sponsored by a friend and/or advisor who is part of the old-boy network and can open doors for her.

The College Grad — She is just out of school, aged from 25 to 35. She has begun lining up her own business contacts and believes she has a network of her own.

The Re-Entry Entrepreneur — She is 41 to 55 and is suddenly on her own through divorce, the death of her spouse, or the empty-nest syndrome. High profits may not be her priority as much as getting back into the thick of things.

It seems appropriate to add a category for unemployed women, as well as one for those with an incredibly wonderful idea. Regardless of your category, let's take a look at what you bring to your venture.

Self-Assessment

Entrepreneurship takes self-knowledge. Since most of us will perceive our traits and abilities positively, be careful when you are assessing yourself to be as honest as possible. The scoring method simply makes you aware of your particular abilities at this time in your life.

Rate yourself in the following areas using this point system:

1. I am convinced this trait does not apply to me.
2. I feel it may be possible to cultivate this trait in myself.
3. I display this trait sometimes.
4. I display this trait most of the time.
5. I always display this trait.

TRAIT	SCORE 1	2	3	4	5
Independence					
Analytical ability					
Achievement orientation					
Perseverance					
Competitiveness					
Good health					
Creativity/Innovation					
Risk-taking					
Self-confidence					
High energy level					
Social skills					
Intuitive skills					

Now that you have identified strengths and weaknesses from the entrepreneurial trait checklist, let's take a closer look at each.

Independence is the hallmark of the entrepreneur. An entrepreneur must have the ability to work alone. Ardith Scrutton, owner of A.J. Copyrite Printing and Typesetting in Halifax, says it all: "I couldn't think of anyone other than myself I would like to work for." Long after their ventures have been launched, many entrepreneurs can attest to the long hours of solitary dedication during the start-up years.

Analytical ability is essential in order to assess the reasons for the success or failure of a venture. I asked small-business lawyer Yvonne Chenier if she had an opinion on the need for entrepreneurial analytical ability. She did. "It's the only way you can be successful," said Chenier, president of four-year-old, Calgary-based Chenier and Company.

Achievement orientation is no longer a dirty phrase for women. Today's women are out to make money, take on challenges, and experience that sense of accomplishment that only achievement can provide. This has been documented in the spirited *Men Are Just Desserts* by Dr. Sonya Friedman. Or in the words of Shirley MacLaine, accepting her Oscar for *Terms of Endearment,* "Thank you. I earned it."

Perseverance is the ability — and I strongly suspect it is also the need — to keep trying when others would not. In 1977 Judy Einarson, a Saskatoon life insurance agent with four children, decided she wanted to be her own boss. With money from a variety of sources, she purchased a 30-year-old trucking business then grossing $365,000 a year. Her advice to other entrepreneurs: "Set your goals and strive to survive, regardless of setbacks. Don't be discouraged by refusals of money or support. Be tenacious."

Competitiveness is a quality widely regarded as masculine according to authors Margaret Hennig and Anne Jardim in *The Managerial Woman.* Further, "fundamental requirements for succeeding at anything include the drive to achieve, orientation to task, the desire to be respected for one's abilities, the enjoyment of competition," and "a capacity to take risk." Multi-millionaire real estate mogul Frances Olson of Calgary advises entrepreneurial women to "assume that a failure would be catastrophic — call it the courage of desperation, but make it work *for* you."

Good health is essential to the success of your venture. The new demands and responsibilities of a business will necessitate an honest, thorough exploration of your present lifestyle and a healthy body to cope with increased stress. The career change to entrepreneurship will inevitably affect your family, friends, and leisure time. The authors of *Women's Burnout,* Dr. Herbert J. Freudenberger and Gail North, identify twelve stages of Women's Burnout: the Compulsion to Prove, Intensity, Subtle Deprivations, Dismissal of Conflict, Distortion of Values, Heightened Denial, Disengagement, Observable Behaviour Changes, Depersonalization, Emptiness, Depression, and Total Burnout. "The degree of intensity and length of time one stays in any particular stage is dependent upon personality, self-perception, previous history, and your ability to cope with stress." Some known stressbusters are exercise, yoga, meditation, and visualization. Whatever technique you choose, be aware always that stress will take its toll on your health, and your business, if not carefully monitored.

Creativity and innovation are the seeds of any new venture. An entrepreneur is the creator of a new enterprise. Nobel Prize-winning physician Albert Szent-Györgyi put it this way: "Discovery consists of looking at the same thing as everyone else and thinking something different." During the run of your entrepreneurial experience you will be called upon to look at a situation creatively in order to change its dimensions or give it new focus. It may mean a shift in company goals, policies, target market, or even the business itself. Sometimes it is the creativity or talent of a woman that will propel her into business for herself. Frequently, women indicate that their reason for going into business is to make use of an unexplored talent or ability.

"Private women inventors [those not inventing on behalf of a corporation] mostly deal with household things and children. There are not a lot of women engineers," Gary Svoboda, a market analyst at the Waterloo, Ontario, Innovation Centre told Linda Hossie of the Toronto *Globe and Mail.* But Dr. Diana Mitchell, a Vancouver psychologist and inventor, is an exception to the rule. Launched this year is a plastic chair-like device which supports reinforcing steel bars in concrete buildings. "The biggest challenge was in designing the chair to avoid any other patent application. The device is usable only once, then gets thrown away," says Mitchell, beaming.

Risk-taking ability is a quality an entrepreneur must have for a variety of reasons. To start with, the fact that there are no guarantees of profit or success in business creation calls for a type of individual who can live with the unknown. The need for people to take risks to meet the challenge of the eighties has given rise to seminars on the subject by Toronto entrepreneur, Reva Nelson, of Words Worth. She cautions, "It's important to take risks out of strength, not weakness. You have to acknowledge that you want to change, weigh the options, and move into problem solving and decision making."

Self-confidence is absolutely necessary. Without the ability to tackle problems head-on, and with a firm sense of self-worth, you'll find yourself like so many leaves scattered in the wind. Although new entrepreneurs need this character trait when they start a venture, I have yet to discover one who has not experienced a manifold increase in self-confidence as she successfully realized her dream.

Energy level had better be high if you are going to be an entrepreneur, particularly if you have a husband and children. Lucky is the woman entrepreneur whose husband will assume some of the domestic responsibilities. I know of many women business owners who actually employ their teenage children to perform tasks such as delivering flyers, taking surveys at shopping malls, and "go-fering" around town, rather than using expensive courier services. Some women simply have to revamp their entire lives, as did one Calgarian, Leanne Forest, owner of the Enchanted Forest Christmas and Gift Shop which specializes in Christmas decorations for home and street. She wrote, "With a great deal of juggling and prioritizing, anything is possible. But it does get hairy sometimes."

Social skills are an asset on many levels. Sophisticated human relations will be necessary to deal with everyone from your staff to your suppliers to the bank. The ability to work well with others and to give and gain cooperation from your employees and associates can make or break a business. For example, Aanderra Systems, a thriving Vancouver Island corporation headed by Gayle Gable, manufactures high-tech marine biology equipment. Gable attributes the company's success in part to her ability to "hire topnotch people and keep a good crew."

Intuitive skills we all possess. What is different amongst us is our ability to trust those instincts or impulses. Men call it "a gut feeling." Some people prefer "following their noses," as one *Financial Times* writer, Elaine Wyatt, put it, and that facility serves them well. Wilma Stewart, for example, had seen the children's crèches in Europe and was disappointed by the care of children in Canada. She says, according to Wyatt, "Daycare was care-giving with a little bit of programming. I do it the other way around." Her Halifax Children's Corner Daycare Centre now has a six-month waiting list. The ability to perceive what is needed instinctively, and the *chutzpah* to make it happen, are traits shared by entrepreneurs all over the world.

Your Attitude

Entrepreneurial traits and tendencies have a lot to do with attitude. When Halifax Business Academy owner Marie Watters walked out on her high school teaching job muttering to herself, "I'll start my own damn school," she was a newly divorced mother of three. It was her positive attitude that really turned on the entrepreneurial light for her $500,000 business academy. While working at twenty part-time secretarial jobs, she took the opportunity to interview employers about their staffs. She soon realized that a business school needed to teach more than skills; it needed to teach attitude. In her spare time Watters renovated her run-down house with a $5,000 down payment borrowed from her mother, and another $5,000 from the bank, and built a suite in the basement to help pay the mortgage. Two years later the house was sold and the academy was launched. That was ten years ago. Then, as now, 95 per cent of her graduates find jobs immediately. A good portion of what the academy provides is confidence and support. At 59, Watters exudes confidence. Who wouldn't — the chance she took was done against the advice of both her lawyer and accountant. It is a common entrepreneurial trait to feel you can do things better than others can. It is this belief in self that will give you the courage to hang in when the times get tough.

Going into business for yourself, regardless of the reason, can be valid if you honestly answer "yes" to the following:

1. You know the business inside and out or have a partner/associate who does.
2. You have carefully mapped out your business plan, marketing plan, and cashflow for a minimum of six months.
3. You have done your homework and have established the fact that there is a market for your product or service.
4. You have the commitment and the burning desire to make the business a success.
5. You have made use of professionals and have obtained a clear-cut picture of financial and legal implications.
6. You have the ability to surround yourself with success and are willing to network with people who are in a position to help you.

7. You are willing to pay the price emotionally, financially, and spiritually.

Of course, you have answered "yes" to all of the above. There's something in the entrepreneurial spirit that keeps it positive through all kinds of start-up decisions. As a matter of fact, Phil O'Brien, president of the Montreal Chamber of Commerce, calls entrepreneurs "today's heroes." Molly Maid founder Adrienne Stringer of Oakville, Ontario, disillusioned with nursing, came to the conclusion that "there had to be a better way to make money." Although Stringer sold 80 per cent of her company to current Molly Maid president James MacKenzie, her original concept has skyrocketed into the largest home-cleaning service in the world, now international in scope. Not bad for a $1,500 investment.

Sounds encouraging, right? But first things first. What you need to do is to determine whether or not you are an entrepreneurial candidate. If you have successfully undertaken the analysis of your skills outlined above, try this next.

Networking

Interview a woman entrepreneur who has successfully launched the type of business you would like to have. Spend about one hour with her, and as you are listening for her honesty as well as her commitment to success, assess yourself. Ask yourself three critical questions:

1. Is this what I want?
2. Is this what I need?
3. Am I willing to pay the price financially, emotionally, and spiritually?

Try the following interview questions:

1. Did you come from an entrepreneurial background or at least know first-hand a number of successful entrepreneurs?
2. What was your reason for starting a business?
3. Did you have business experience in the area of your enterprise?
4. How were you most and how were you least prepared for your venture?

5. Did you have financial reserves to fall back on in the event your venture failed?
6. How did you obtain your financing?
7. How did you research your market?
8. Did you have emotional support from family and friends?
9. How has entrepreneurship affected your immediate family?
10. Do you now see yourself as a success? In what way?
11. How has success changed you?
12. How closely have you stuck to your original business goals?
13. In what ways do you feel you were prepared for business? In what ways do you feel you were unprepared for business?
14. What do you feel would be the single most helpful piece of advice you can give me?
15. If you had to do it all over again, would you? Why? Why not?

For some, this interview may represent the end of the road. For others, it will encourage you as well as reconfirm your belief in your chances of success. Frequently women come away from this exercise with a new sense of personal insight. Some even determine ways in which they can run the business better than they would have otherwise.

Now is your chance to really have fun. Make use of a very good friend (someone you trust and who is supportive of your career goals) and have them interview you as though you were already a successful woman entrepreneur. Have them ask you the same questions you asked your role model. Keep in mind the fact that success in your business has already been established. Allow yourself to fantasize! You may be surprised at some of the answers jumping from your subconscious. One Toronto woman I know found that the more she talked, the more she talked herself right out of business ownership. She could not quite put herself into the position of success. Her family came first — the price was simply too high. The exercise can, of course, work in an opposite and reconfirming way, as in the case of a woman who painted her own success scenario so vividly that she became more determined than ever that this was the route for her. Both women came out winners. Both decided for themselves what was truly important and were honestly able to assess the probable price of success for them.

What Entrepreneurship Holds for Me

Now try this exercise. Review the list below and then start building your personal list of the positive as well as negative aspects of going into business for yourself. This list is by no means complete, but it should get you going.

Positive

a chance to be my own boss
freedom to create my own level of income
freedom to be challenged
freedom from the threat of dismissal
job satisfaction
increased feeling of self-worth
freedom to choose goals
flexible work hours
flexible work location
choice of work atmosphere
choice of work
freedom
power

Negative

little income for the first few years
less time with my family and friends
the necessity of risk-taking
long hours
impact on close personal relationships
possible loss of friends
initial lack of company benefits
increased stress
very limited time off; hours at client's convenience
responsibility for self-motivation
no work — no money
loneliness
sacrifice

A Basic Entrepreneurial Start-Up Quiz

The following quiz will help to identify some of your own

entrepreneurial characteristics. It is taken from William Jennings's *Entrepreneurship: A Primer for Canadians.*

1. Faced with a problem, the entrepreneur is most likely to:
   a. go to a close friend for help.
   b. get help from a stranger who is known to be an expert.
   c. try to work through the problem alone.
2. The entrepreneur is most like the distance runner who runs mainly:
   a. to work off energy and to keep in good physical condition.
   b. to gain the satisfaction of beating other competitors in the race.
   c. to try to better her previous time over the distance.
3. Entrepreneurs are motivated most by the need to:
   a. achieve a goal of great personal importance.
   b. gain public attention and recognition.
   c. control wealth and other people.
4. Entrepreneurs believe the success or failure of a new business venture depends primarily upon:
   a. luck or fate.
   b. the support and approval of others.
   c. their own strengths and abilities.
5. If given the chance to earn a substantial reward, which of the following would entrepreneurs be most likely to do:
   a. roll dice with a one-in-three chance of winning.
   b. work on a problem with a one-in-three chance of solving it in the time given.
   c. do neither (a) nor (b) because the chances of success are so small.
6. The entrepreneur is most likely to choose a task:
   a. that involves a moderate level of risk but is still challenging.
   b. where the risks are high but the financial rewards are also very great.
   c. that is relatively easy and low-risk.
7. Profits are important to entrepreneurs because:
   a. profits provide the money that allows them to develop other ideas and take advantage of other opportunities.

   b. profits are an objective measure of how successful they have been.
   c. the main reason they accepted the risks of starting a new business was to accumulate personal wealth (make a big profit).
8. Entrepreneurs value most highly in their jobs:
   a. the importance placed on competence and efficiency.
   b. the freedom to control how they use their time.
   c. the opportunity to create and to do new things.

Answers: 1.b, 2.c, 3.a, 4.c, 5.b, 6.a, 7.a or b, 8.c.

Your Personal History

If you passed the quiz with flying colours, it's time to use your past to help determine your future. Those of you with a healthy amount of current business experience will probably have a fairly good idea of what business is for you. Those who have been out of the workplace for a number of years may need a little self-analysis to help identify skills and preferences. One woman told me that "mine is a modest one-man-band operation providing a service to the oil industry. I spent a long period raising children and went back to my profession to see my contemporaries in senior management positions. My own business gives me strokes, independence, and flexibility as well as better remuneration than I would have as an employee of a large company."

Let's take a look at an exercise adapted from Sandra Winston's book *The Entrepreneurial Woman.* Think of your life in terms of five-year blocks of time, beginning at the age of 15. On a separate sheet of paper for each five-year block (15-20, 20-25, 25-30, 30-35), ask yourself the following questions:

1. What were my hobbies?
2. How did I do in school?
3. What did I excel in?
4. What did I enjoy?
5. Did I have a job? If so, doing what?
6. What extracurricular activities did I take part in?
7. What about sports? How involved was I?
8. What environment did I best enjoy?
9. Did I like to be inside or outside?

10. Did I like to be with people or alone?
11. Did I prefer the country or the city?

Next, using a separate sheet of paper for each question above, use the following as headings:

WHAT I DID
WHERE I DID IT
WHAT I LIKED ABOUT IT
WHAT I DID NOT LIKE ABOUT IT

Finally, list on a separate sheet of paper those things you liked doing. Look at these events, activities, or circumstances to determine your direction in choosing a business.

Your Comfort Zone

One more step in your self-assessment is an exercise providing you with choices you may never have considered before. In this exercise you will have the opportunity to identify six fields of endeavour. Most people come up with a combination of two or three. While making your decisions, try to recall past as well as current experiences. In the exercise below, identify fields of endeavour in which you feel most comfortable.

1. You have athletic or mechanical ability, preferring to work with objects, machines, tools, plants, or animals. Perhaps you like to work outdoors.
   What experience have you had in this area?
   How can you use that experience in the creation of a business?
2. You like to work with data, have clerical or numerical ability, enjoy organizing details, and possess good follow-up ability.
   What experience have you had in this area?
   How can you use that experience in the creation of a business?
3. You like to work with people — influencing, persuading, or performing, leading or managing.
   What experience have you had in this area?
   How can you use that experience in the creation of a business?
4. You like to work with people to inform, enlighten, help, train, or develop. You could also be skilled with words.
   What experience have you had in this area?
   How can you use that experience in the creation of a business?

5. You have artistic, inventive, innovative abilities. You are usually highly intuitive and enjoy making use of your imagination or creativity.
   What experience have you had in this area?
   How can you use that experience in the creation of a business?
6. You like to observe, learn, investigate, analyze, evaluate, or solve problems.
   What experience have you had in this area?
   How can you use that experience in the creation of a business?

It is important that you be honest with yourself. I have never talked with a successful woman entrepreneur who did not love her work and who was not able to provide a safe, comfortable environment for herself. If you know your strengths as well as your weaknesses, you are better able to capitalize on those strengths and devise a plan of action to correct the weaknesses. That plan of action may take the form of courses, a partnership, creation of a venture you may not have considered, or rethinking your business.

Michelle Allen of Extraordinary Casting, Inc. in Vancouver, puts it this way: "All the job tasks I have ever performed have been valuable to my business. They taught me how to deal with the public — diplomacy, patience, discipline, professionalism — many things." When you consider Allen's background — waitress, professional singer, secretary, salesclerk, production assistant — she could have chosen a number of directions. Allen's company provides a much-needed service supplying walk-ons and extras to the motion picture industry. When Hollywood came north to shoot pictures, there was no agency to supply performers other than those agencies which handled actors in major roles or with specialized talents. Her business now casts exclusively for major motion pictures. What Allen knew about herself was that she was disciplined, had creative insight, and loved to work with bright, creative motion picture people.

The Business for You

Finding the right business may be one of the biggest challenges you have ever faced. Some people know instinctively, some give in to a long-held fantasy, some base their decision on previous work experience. One such woman had just finished her Masters in Education when Evelyn Woods Reading Dynamics of Halifax went looking for a part-time instructor. Ilene Peece knew speed reading worked, but was having real difficulty convincing some of her academic peers that it was more than a passing fad. Divorced and the mother of children aged two and four, she came to the conclusion that, "I would have to support myself for the rest of my life and I wouldn't be able to develop a new business by myself." What she *was* able to capitalize on was the fact that she was the only person east of Montreal who had the qualifications to teach speed reading. Eventually, her former employer went bankrupt and Peece developed her own speed-reading course. In the summer of 1986 she hired an MBA student to help her get a business and financial orientation on the direction of the company. Still working out of her home, she managed to make in six months a salary that the majority of Canadians don't make in a year. With the help of her student and the achievement of her five-year objectives, she will be able to determine who else, other than reading teachers and professors, can be included in her target market, and so expand the business.

Capitalizing on Trends

Then there are those who have already made their decision and simply adapt, or women who actually choose their business based on what the academic community calls forecasting, or trends. Some people call it plain "good timing." Whatever you call it, you will seriously diminish your chances of success if you don't notice what is going on around you.

Let's look at how paying attention to trends and fads and the fickle behaviour of the Canadian consumer may point you in the direction of success. For example, five women living in three different parts of the country have created businesses based on the baby boomer's baby boom. According to a Toronto research executive quoted in the *Financial Times,* "sales of goods and services aimed at pregnant women in Canada could add up to a staggering $1 billion a year." Apparently, there is at least another decade to go before this generation is finished childbearing, so if you're planning to tap the market, do it now.

Miriam Parker, founder and owner of Toronto's Preggae Woman, holds thirty exercise classes for pregnant women each week, at four locations. She estimates 600 pregnant women attended her classes last year, each spending an average of $300 to $400. Parker, herself pregnant, is ready to franchise. "The potential is enormous," she says. "It's like the funeral business. You're guaranteed that people are going to get pregnant." She ought to know; since we first talked, she has had *another* baby.

On the west coast, Libby Ordel, president of The Ordel Group, along with partner Marilyn Taylor, stages an annual consumer show called "Babies in the Eighties," complete with corporate sponsorship and beautiful-baby contests. Ordel's business is promotion — she pays attention to trends and makes use of her creativity. The company she created was bought out by her partner at a considerable profit to Ordel.

Then there's Stork Express, owned by two Ottawa women, Joy Kardish and Joanne Phillips, who personally deliver gift baskets to new mothers and babies at prices ranging from $20 to $200. They amuse themselves as well as their clients by dressing in stork costumes. Between the two of them they have seven children. They have found a way to manage families while fulfilling their desire to go into business.

The importance of the baby boomers in the marketplace is considerable. In 1986 the 353,000 Canadians born in 1946 turned 40. And according to University of Waterloo statistics quoted in the Vancouver *Sun,* "the big wave is still to come. Those now reaching forty have been labelled the cutting edge of the baby boom. The real baby boom years were 1952 to 1966 (boomers now aged 20 to 34)." It seems they're in better physical health, drink and smoke less, and worry more about cholesterol and fat. Their attention has gone to lifestyle issues — the women's movement, male sensitivity, their 1.4 children, and consumer debt.

It is important for you to be aware of this consumer group's spending habits and belief systems, to know, for example, that they've caused real estate prices to skyrocket because there are so many of them with disposable income. From that information it is possible to identify myriad businesses. For example, possible classes you may want to teach include: parenting, pre-natal and post-natal care (including exercising and diet), coping with post-partum depression, effective real estate investing, investing for couples (or women or men), healthy cooking, how to stop smoking, how to feel good about being 40, and on and on. Any one of these, put into the hands of the right entrepreneur, could turn into a bona fide business.

Let's take a look at more trends offered in *Small Business* by Bob Johnson. "It often seems that the only prediction we can make with certainty is that the future will be uncertain. But there are social, economic, and moral trends now emerging that can help us create a more reassuring vision of the future." Women who start businesses require vision. The vision will launch the enterprise, allow it to adapt, change, re-direct, and survive. One trend Johnson talks about is no surprise to anyone — new technology. People who have managed to survive the recession in highly competitive businesses, such as employment agencies, have needed to pay attention to trends.

Barbara Rae, a twenty-year veteran of the employment agency business, uses a local FM radio station not only to promote her business, but also to keep listeners informed about the world of office automation. With sales close to $15 million a year, Rae's Office Assistance Canada Limited is the largest permanent and temporary office placement firm in western Canada.

Other trends can be traced by identifying age clusters, according to Johnson's article. By defining two clusters as significant factors, we can be alerted to business opportunities and threats for the future. "For example," says Johnson, "the number of Canadians aged 35-49 will grow by 33 per cent by 1995. . . . These days, both partners in a relationship often earn high salaries, and spend their money on everything from kayaks to quiche."

"The impact of the working woman," emphasizes noted futurist and author of *Megatrends,* John Naisbitt, in an article in *The Franchise Handbook,* "on the creation of new services cannot be overstated. Specifically, a desire for convenience has spawned an array of franchises offering services traditionally performed by stay-at-home women.'' The two-career family will create the need for everything from daycare to home and lawn care, dry cleaning and personal services. The other end of the demographics deserves equal attention. You can bet the need for home-call nurses will increase with the increased senior population, as will exercise classes geared to the elderly. The age group 65 and older has significantly more women than men; more than 90 per cent live in private households; and by the year 2000, low-income widows will predominate at this end of the age spectrum. Merchants will need to be more sensitive to the needs of older customers. This fastest-growing segment of society will need to be ``courted consumers'' as they have more disposable income than any other group.

The new emphasis on fitness has helped propel The Fitness Group's president, Barbara Crompton, into a position of leadership in the field. She appeals both to individuals willing to take responsibility for their own fitness, and to corporations concerned about employee fitness.

Trends can be determined from a variety of sources such as public libraries, Chambers of Commerce, Statistics Canada, and all levels of government. There are small, privately produced reports, like Lynda J. Jackson's *Financial Planning Report* (Canadian economic, personal financial planning, and investment trends) from Vancouver; and of course, the biggie, America's most prestigious (and expensive), the *Kiplinger Washington Letter* (1729 H St. N.W., Washington, D.C. 20006, USA).

Getting Specific

Keeping trends in mind, complete this exercise. First, add your own job ideas to the list quickly, randomly, and without judgement or consideration. Then go back and put checkmarks first beside those businesses that may be of interest and then under the appropriate headings for each.

BUSINESS	I see myself doing this job.	I have the skill to do it.	I have the ability to learn this skill.	I have talent for this type of work.	I have experience in this work.
Dressmaker					
Folk artist					
Talent agent					
Promoter					
Bookkeeper					
Colour coordinator					
Office plant specialist					
Sandwich business					
Knitwear designer					
Antique furniture dealer/restorer					
House sitter					
Pet walker					
Letter-writing service					
Retail store owner					
Consultant					
Copywriting					
Typing					
Child photography					
Tutoring					
Pet limo service					
Professional shopper					
Data processor					
Mobile mechanic					
Cabinetmaker					
House builder					
Publisher					
Going it alone in my profession					

Management Skills

Now that you have a fairly good idea of which business is for you, one of the most important criteria must be addressed—your management experience. Doreen Braverman, owner of Vancouver's The Flag Shop, says that "a good housewife can handle ten things at the same time." If that's not management, I don't know what is. Use the following checklist as an indicator of your management expertise. You will note that two areas of your life are addressed: management at home and management on the job. Rate yourself 1 through 4 as follows:

1. Not one of my skills.
2. I do this well sometimes.
3. I do this well most of the time.
4. I do this well all of the time.

	AT HOME				ON THE JOB			
	1	2	3	4	1	2	3	4
I am good at problem solving/decision making.								
I handle stress well.								
I am good at sharing and delegating work.								
I have a network of business contacts.								
I can meet deadlines and prioritize.								
I am good at effective time management.								
I adhere to goals.								
I have a good management style.								
I have good communications skills, both written and oral.								
I am good at budgeting.								
I am good at policy making.								
I have the ability to set an example and lead.								
I am good at building a team.								

If you determine that your management skills are very limited, it does not necessarily mean that you should give up your dream. It does, however, mean that you should consider holding off on your dream until you have acquired skills, either through courses or related job experience, have found a partner who has the skills, or can hire someone to fill the void.

Before You Start

If the above self-assessment encouraged you to go into business for yourself, look at it as the first of many steps necessary to ensure entrepreneurial success. The road to success starts with planning those steps. As an entrepreneur it will be your responsibility to organize your venture. It will take keen organizational ability and sound management to ensure not only your salary but a profit as well. While being the boss lets you put your feet up on the desk, take three-hour lunches, and carry a lizardskin briefcase, you also have work to do. First of all, how are you going to finance the venture? What form will your business take?

It may be helpful to take note of some of the problems experienced by other women as first-time business owners. Among frequently heard comments are these:

> "I would have taken sales and business courses before beginning. There isn't time now, because I'm too busy learning about the business."
>
> "It was lonely and difficult being on my own at first. I felt pressured because of being solely responsible for deadlines. I should have considered a partnership to offset work and expenses."
>
> "I would have liked to have studied personnel management and bookkeeping, and taken some computer courses prior to actually starting."
>
> "I would have taken a course in business management instead of flying by the seat of my pants."
>
> "I would have talked to more people operating similar businesses before starting."
>
> "I continue to have difficulty putting a price on services and often give things away. I sometimes feel my female upbringing makes it hard for me to value what I can contribute

to my clients. I find it easier to ask for money from a woman, but whether from male or female, I find it difficult to ask for money."

Your Financial Picture

Since this difficulty in asking for and, in general, dealing with money is not that uncommon, it is important for you to take a serious look at your finances. Long before you start costing out business expenses you must take a realistic look at what money you have, what is available to you, and what your obligations are to date. A good place to start is with a personal balance sheet of net worth. You may want to use the balance sheet provided below as your guide. Next, you would be wise to do an income and expense statement. Again, you may wish to use the guide provided on page 29.

BALANCE SHEET*

Assets: Everything you own with cash value.

Cash: money on hand including bank accounts	$ _____
Stocks, bonds, term deposits, mutual funds	$ _____
RRSP (less tax)	$ _____
Cash value, life insurance, pension	$ _____
Monies owed to you — goods, services, notes	$ _____
Autos, other vehicles	$ _____
Real estate market value	$ _____
Collectibles and antiques	$ _____
Home furnishings, household goods (replacement or cash)	$ _____
Jewellery and furs	$ _____
Other ______________________	$ _____
TOTAL ASSETS	$ _____

Liabilities: Your debts.

Time payments, credit cards, lay-aways	$ _____

* To be used in conjunction with the Income & Expense Statement if you are presently employed by someone else; otherwise, use by itself.

Contracts payable (includes balance on car, boat, furniture, or services)	$ ______
Notes payable	$ ______
Taxes outstanding	$ ______
Mortgage(s)	$ ______
Insurance premiums outstanding	$ ______
Other ____________________________	$ ______
TOTAL LIABILITIES	$ ______

To establish your net worth, subtract your liabilities from your assets.

Assets	$ ______
Less Liabilities	$ ______
NET WORTH	$ ______

INCOME AND EXPENSE STATEMENT*

Income: Money you receive for your use.

Gross salary/wage	$ ______	
Less deductions	$ ______	
Take home pay		$ ______
Spouse salary/wage or other income	$ ______	
Less deductions	$ ______	
Take home pay		$ ______
Rental income		$ ______
Commissions, bonuses		$ ______
Child support, maintenance		$ ______
Interest and dividends		$ ______
Pension, annuities		$ ______
Trusts, royalties, residuals		$ ______
Miscellaneous		$ ______
TOTAL INCOME		$ ______
Total Income		$ ______
Less Total Expenses (Fixed and Variable)		$ ______
Monthly Surplus		$ ______

---

* To be used only if you are still employed by someone else.

Fixed Expenses: Payments you must make at regular times for fixed amounts.	
Rent or mortgage	$ ______
Property taxes, if not Principal, interest and taxes	$ ______
Installment contract payments	$ ______
Regular payments to others, church, charities	$ ______
Insurance	$ ______
Income taxes	$ ______
Dues, memberships	$ ______
Total Fixed Expenses	$ ______

Variable Expenses: Regular expenses that may vary from month to month.	
Utilities: gas, electricity, phone, cable, etc.	$ ______
Medical/dental	$ ______
Transportation: gas, oil, parking, taxi	$ ______
Household maintenance	$ ______
Child care	$ ______
Food and groceries	$ ______
Personal maintenance	$ ______
Self-improvement/education	$ ______
Recreation/entertainment	$ ______
Total Variable Expenses	$ ______

Start-Up Costs

Just as you will have variable and fixed costs personally, so will your business. Before a single dollar crosses your palm, your business will incur expenses. You may need a lawyer, accountant, business licence, office equipment, rent, furniture, telephone or utility hook-up — all payable in advance — just for starters.

In two studies of women business owners in Canada, one by The Royal Bank of Canada and one by Laventhol & Horwath, it has been determined that Canadian women generally start their enterprises with funds in the vicinity of $10,000 to $12,000. At this stage of planning you should be looking at what you personally can contribute financially to your business before seeking outside help. Use the Balance Sheet provided to determine how much liquidity you have right now.

If you are currently employed, your next step is to determine how much it will cost to launch the business. Perhaps you have enough money already. If not, you will need to secure financing from outside sources such as family, friends, a loan, or venture capital. Many would-be entrepreneurs decide to remain employed long enough to cover outstanding financial obligations, put aside a six-month salary, and provide sufficient start-up capital for the venture. A word of caution: if you are currently employed, decide to go ahead with a business, and know you will need a loan from a financial institution, that loan will in all probability be executed as a personal one, so get the loan before you quit the job.

Research has indicated that women are generally more prudent in their financial management than men. Could it be that we are used to coping with less because we are paid less, that we have had occasion to balance a family budget, or is it that our general philosophy concerning money is different? Elaine Wyatt in the *Financial Times* quotes Judith Andrew, associate director of research with the Canadian Federation of Independent Business, who says that men tend to be significantly more optimistic and more likely to be impulsive in business. Women, it seems, are "flooding into business seminars and management courses."

I suppose *prudent* is a good word to describe Barbara Caldwell's launch into her $1.8-million Cleanwear Products Ltd. in Scarborough, Ontario. Her business, the manufacturing of sterile disposable clothing for the pharmaceutical, nuclear, and food-processing industries, is a far cry from her initial investment of 5,000 yards of cloth.

Another of the reasons why women's business survival rate is higher than men's is that we tend to do our homework. We're willing to invest several months in planning beforehand. Some of this planning time should go into evaluating Smart and Not-So-Smart Financial Risks. Jeanette Scollard, in her book *The Self-Employed Woman,* refers to them as "Foolish versus Intelligent" risks. Whatever you call them, running a business calls for keen decision making. The following is a guideline for Smart and Not-So-Smart Financial Risk-Taking.

Risk-Taking for the Beginner

SMART RISKS

1. Assume or start a business you thoroughly enjoy.
2. Overestimate your operating costs. It will be difficult to get another loan or a larger line of credit. Investors might assume you have not done your homework thoroughly.
3. Know your market thoroughly. Know your competition and charge a going rate. It is dangerous to set a precedent, particularly in the case of a consultancy, for example, by underpricing.
4. Pay yourself a salary you can afford. It may not be as high as your last job, but it should keep you afloat. Many entrepreneurs do not pay themselves for the first year. While this practice is widespread, it is not good psychologically.
5. Never take the public for granted. Place service, integrity, and honesty high among your priorities.
6. Keep up-to-the minute relations with your banker. Keep your commitments and always be on the lookout for sources of capital for future growth.
7. Assess your credit policy very carefully. Know that not everyone will pay on time or, for that matter, pay at all.
8. Get professional help in preparing your business plan and cashflow chart, particularly when your business is retail and there are many projections to be made.
9. Hire someone who has different skills, abilities, and characteristics than you. It is smart to pay attention to your gut feelings or intuition when hiring staff. Look around carefully for that first person you hire. In your absence, they *are* your business.
10. Define the employee's job with a job description and make sure he or she understands his or her obligations. Be willing to delegate.
11. Understand your market enough (as in the case of a consulting business) to determine if location will be a consideration. Needless to say, in retail or manufacturing, location is critical. Working out of the home may be acceptable to your clientele and may eliminate the need for a nanny.

12. Join clubs and associations for new businesses and muster support for your new enterprise. Don't throw away supporters and friends as you become successful. Smart entrepreneurs know that at any time they could be forced to start all over again.
13. Define your business goals. This exercise will enhance your chances of success, as will a system of time management.
14. Ascertain and adhere to local, provincial, and federal requirements regarding everything from zoning to business licences.
15. Fulfill provincial and federal taxation requirements. Know what is required and live up to obligations.
16. Know how to elicit the help of family, friends, spouse, children, and anyone else who will help you with your enterprise.
17. Use courses, libraries, industry magazines, and related publications.

NOT-SO-SMART RISKS

1. Assume or start a business you do not like. Base your decision to become an entrepreneur solely on the ability of the venture to make money.
2. Pretend you have more start-up funds than you really have. Underestimate the costs of office supplies and salary, so the lending institution will think it is taking less of a risk.
3. Assume that because your product or service costs less than your competition's, people will flock to your door.
4. Pay yourself what you made working for someone else, or better.
5. Feel convinced that once you have someone's business, it will always be yours. Expect customer loyalty before it is earned.
6. Communicate with your banker only after you have run out of money and manage your cashflow on an ad hoc basis. If you need extra capital your first choice would be to bring in a partner with cash.
7. Spend your working capital down to the last dollar in the belief that your receivables will be in on time to pay your suppliers and the rent.

8. Assume that you have considered every possible cost and detail that investors, or others willing to lend you money, will want to see. Assume that people who do not cut corners are not smart.
9. Hire someone with your background and entrepreneurial ambitions. Hire a friend's friend or hire solely on the recommendation of another person. Hire someone because the price is right and because you really don't have time to interview others.
10. Be vague in your employee's job description and frequently change direction. Give employees no decision-making authority, but if anything goes wrong — blame them!
11. Rent the most expensive office space to impress your clients. Do a minimum of comparison shopping for warehouse and manufacturing locations. Ignore the fact that product, pricing, and image will affect your location.
12. Assume that you have achieved success on your own and that you do not need the continued support of your friends and colleagues. Forget how important these people were when you needed them most.
13. Fly by the seat of your pants, without goals or time management plans.
14. Assume that no one will know or that it does not make a difference if you obey the law or not. Invest in site conversion or leasehold improvements only to be informed of a zoning infraction after the work has been completed.
15. Ignore tax obligations. Assume that you will never be caught.
16. Try to do everything yourself — no matter how much energy you have, or how clever you may be.
17. Launch your venture and become so busy surviving that you are not keeping up with the times.

Four Options

It is important for you at this stage to consider the four entry level options for business ownership. They are: starting from scratch, buying an existing business, franchising, or direct sales. Perhaps the biggest single deciding factor is the amount of money you will need for start-up, but the type of business you undertake is important as well. *Starting from scratch* is what most entrepreneurs like to do. There is something about the challenge of creating the venture that becomes an integral part of the long-term commitment to success that comes with entrepreneurship. The self-assessment, the identification of the market niche, the risk of putting yourself on the line — body, soul, and bank account — to realize a dream is very different from buying an already existing business.

Let's suppose that you have always wanted a boutique. You feel that for one reason or another starting from scratch is a bad move. The second way of realizing your dream is to *buy an existing business.* Whether you locate your potential business based on word-of-mouth disclosures (bankers, suppliers, rumours), on classified newspaper ads, real estate brokers, or trade publications, you are in for a lot of homework.

First of all, talk with the owner. Secure as much information about the business as you can over the phone and then go sleuthing. Check out the competition, available products and prices, suppliers' prices, and the premises. Go incognito — pretend you are simply a customer. Get a sense of the business. How does the owner treat the customers? Are they likely to come back? Look at the traffic, the location, the condition of the premises. If the opportunity still looks good, make a formal appointment and ask for documentation, including financial statements, the lease, and any promotional material describing the business's products or services. First and foremost, find out why the business is being sold. Is the business too taxing? Is there not enough business? Are supplies difficult to get? Are the accounts receivable too high? It may be a good idea to pay for advice from a business broker, accountant, or banker at this stage. Keep in mind that whenever a business is sold, there are two evaluations placed on it: that of the seller and that of the buyer.

The third method of entry is by *franchising*. Basically, it is an ongoing, contractual agreement between two parties, the franchisor and the franchisee. Franchisors grant the right to market their product or service for a set initial fee, plus royalties. Perhaps the biggest advantage of buying a franchise is that all the groundwork has been done for you. One word of caution: see a lawyer specializing in franchising, and don't assume just because you get to sail under someone else's corporate flag that you've got it made.

While the franchisor may provide advertising for you, the franchisee has to produce the profit.

A fourth type of business ownership is *direct sales.* Whether it's real estate or life insurance, women do exceptionally well in sales. You might want to consider it because of the low initial investment and the chance to test your "people prowess." In 1985, according to Diane Forrest, writing in *Chatelaine,* more than 275,000 Canadians earned all or a portion of their income by knocking on doors or holding home parties. We sold everything from lingerie to hydroponic plant equipment. And 85 per cent of the salespeople were women. The biggest advantage is probably the time flexibility.

Some people try direct sales to supplement a sagging salary, while others use it as a money-making project for both spouses, giving them something in common. Then there are those who use direct sales as a way to test their own marketing ability. You will get some degree of training, support, and know-how from the parent company and may or may not have to meet a quota. For those who respond to bonus systems, there's always the pink Cadillac from Mary Kay, or discounts on lingerie, to help push the sales figures higher. How much you earn depends on your ability to sell, on the product, on the commission structure, and on how hard you are willing to work.

One example is Rhya Lornie of Victoria, B.C. A twenty-year veteran of the cosmetics industry, and former employee of Lancôme and Orlane beauty products, Lornie went the direct-selling route ten years ago. With a husband and two children at home, her new career keeps her away from home more than she would like. She has to promote her line, sign up new members, and regularly take courses to keep abreast of the latest trends. But the job does provide her with a $70,000-plus yearly income, and the type of personal freedom she requires.

How do you determine which direct-sales product is for you? Consider what you buy and what you like and appreciate. If you're a gourmet cook, why not consider Tupperware? If you're always finding yourself knee-deep in mud, maybe hydroponic garden kits will provide a way to garden all year round, and help your friends while you're at it. Most women care about clothes and makeup;

find out what products are available that you would feel confident selling.

Who Should Work at Home?

Your decision to run a business from the home or elsewhere will depend to a large degree on the type of business it is. Obviously, your home may not be suitable for a retail operation because of probable zoning regulations. We've all seen chiropractic, dental, even doctors' practices, with their shingles out in front of what appear to be residential buildings, however. Be sure to check the municipal zoning regulations available at your local city hall. Taking your business down the street, into a commercial or business district, creates the proverbial additional mouth to feed. If your business is consulting, for example, and you choose to rent office space, make sure you can afford the rent for a minimum of six months before signing any lease. And speaking of leases, don't sign anything without having it looked at by a lawyer familiar with contract law. The money you spend up front may save you thousands later. The amount of rent you spend should be based on your ability to pay, the level of prestige needed to attract clients and, of course, your own level of comfort. Don't be afraid to negotiate. In some cities, where landlords are desperate for tenants, several months' rent is free if you sign on the dotted line. While this may be enticing, make sure you can afford to keep up the commitment.

Many professional women — consultants, freelancers, owners of service businesses, as well as home-craft practitioners — operate successfully from the home. In the first place, working at home cuts down expenses (keeping in mind that personal and business money usually comes out of the same pot at the beginning). Secondly, if you have school-age children, it allows you to spend more time with them.

You should know yourself well enough to determine whether you need outside stimulation on a daily basis. Many women, whose work is creative, find the giving and receiving of feedback on a daily basis necessary for their growth. It is a fact, too, that some of us simply cannot stand being at home day after day. You should also consider whether or not clients coming and going from your residence would be an infringement on your privacy. There may also be a safety factor if you are working alone and some of your visitors are male. On the other hand, operating a business out of your home will allow you a tax deduction against income. The amount is determined by pro-rating the total expenses of the residence (rent or mortgage, repairs, maintenance, insurance, utilities) in accordance with the area used for business.

Bookkeeping

According to Evelyn Jacks, director of Education, Urban and Rural Tax Service in Winnipeg, "If you work for yourself or own a small business, you'll have to pay special attention to tax matters." Self-employed income or income from business is defined in the Income Tax Act this way: "A taxpayer's income for a taxation year is his profit thereon for the year." In this case, *profit* means net profit — the gross income of a business less the expenses incurred to earn that income. Jacks cautions, "Consider the performance of your business over the last few years when you claim expenses. Do you have any expectation of profit in the future? . . . How long have you been writing off losses? If you're audited and Revenue Canada cannot see a reasonable expectation of profit in the future, the losses you claimed in earlier years may be disallowed completely. This could result in a tax bill inflated with interest charges and/or penalties." Even though you have an accountant, it will still be your responsibility to keep track of all income and expenses. At the beginning, in the majority of cases, all money will be out of the same pot. But be sure to keep accurate records of business income and operating expenses. In addition to your personal bank account, you will need a special one, just for business.

Now you are ready to deal with detailed plans, starting with time-management strategies and goal-setting for your new venture.

Chapter 2

TIME MANAGEMENT FOR THE KNEE-DEEP

My list sits on my desk looking at me right in the face. I'm constantly interrupted throughout the day, but the list remains, each time giving me a starting place.

Suzanne Fennell,
Marketing and Advertising Consultant

It's 7:00 a.m. Do you know where your lists are? Suzanne Fennell does. She is president of SAF & Associates, providing marketing and promotion expertise for western Canada's largest food and retail chain, Woodwards Stores Ltd. "I depend a lot on my thinking time, which is 5:00 to 7:00 in the morning. This is the time when I make notes while I'm dressing. I add these to the lists I've left on my desk the night before. There is never a doubt in my mind by the time I arrive at the office what needs to be done for the day." Have you graduated to To-Do lists or are you still depending on the backs of match covers and check-out counter receipts to remind you what must be done? One woman I spoke with about lists referred to them as the "underwear of daily life."

How do busy people get organized, anyway? We've all heard the expression, "If you want it done, give it to a busy person." It is a fact that well-organized people are not only able to squeeze more work into their schedule, but also have time for fun. Those who accomplish and those who do not are distinguished by the ability to organize and utilize time superbly. The way we handle our personal time before we own a business is probably a significant indicator of our ability to organize our time once we are in business.

Several years ago a seminar speaker introduced me to the expression, "If you fail to plan, you plan to fail." Frequently I use it as a reminder when I am tempted to let things slide. Time-planning and life-goals consultant Alan Lakein puts it this way: "Time is life. It is irreversible and irreplaceable. To waste your time is to waste your life, but to master your time is to master your life and make the most of it."

Let us consider the juggling act of the woman entrepreneur (particularly the one with children at home). She clearly has duties and responsibilities within the framework of her marriage and her obligations to those children. At the same time, the success or failure of her business venture will depend on her time management, as well as on the physical and mental energy she can commit to the undertaking. One woman from Edmonton told me, simply, "I hired a housekeeper, thank God!" Donna Tink, owner of G.P. Compleat Reader Bookstore & Compleat Reader Annex, admits that "the downs of business are the long hours — they often coincide with family fun time." Miriam Parker, the owner of Preggae Woman, started out actually bringing her infant to business lunches. Luckily, in her line of work it was not the *faux pas* it would have been for a computer consultant. Claims Parker, when asked about the ups and downs of business ownership, "Combining my personal life with my business drive is my greatest challenge. It is a stream of never-ending ambiguity and guilt." To further complicate things, her ex-husband alienated her staff, which took her months to reassemble. She met the challenge by becoming more successful than ever after she left her marriage.

Hilda Tiessen, co-founder and director of marketing for Toronto's Sunwheel, one of the largest and most successful bicycle courier operations in the country, is not married. "However," says Tiessen, "my personal relationships suffered during this time" — her five-year start-up when she "lived and breathed the business." Like Hilda, I am not married, but it is a fact that my need to accomplish and grow has, over the years, cost me friends, both male and female.

The most interesting quotation on time management came from clinical and consulting psychologist Dr. Diana Mitchell of Vancouver. Dr. Mitchell's work is in therapy, forensic evaluations, and reports to the courts, as well as in industrial evaluations of potential managers. Diana is not only carrying the workload and responsibility for her practice, but is a partner with her husband and four others in a construction/development company, for which she co-invented special equipment. Her system works as follows:

> [Business] has taken a lot of time so I compensate by sleeping five hours a night. I get up at 4:00 and work till 7:30 . . . . when my seven-year-old gets up. We play till 8:45 when I leave for my clinical work at 9:00. Since I work Saturday mornings and one or two nights a week, I work after my son falls asleep. I have a live-in nanny. She does all the housework and chores, including weekday meals. My husband shares childcare and does all household repairs. He and I share equally the leadership position.

And so goes the story of this incredibly well-organized woman. But we all know that not every woman business owner can afford a nanny, nor does she have a husband to share some of the load physically, financially, or psychologically. Says one successful woman whose business was started eighteen years ago: "Time was my enemy because I had three children and no husband any more."

"In a recent survey," reports Knud Jensen, a director of Time Manager International and professor in the School of Business Management at Ryerson Polytechnical Institute in Toronto, "out of 100 business people questioned, 40 cited their inability to spend more time at home as their most worrying pressure."

Author Alan Lakein, in *How to Get Control of Your Time and Your Life,* discusses what he calls "three notorious characters" caught up in dilemmas over control of their time. The *over-organized person* is probably the most easily recognized. She is forever making lists, only to lose them and start all over again. While her whole world revolves around planning in the minutest detail, she is caught in her own game, because there is no time left for the execution of her plans. We have all known the type of people identified as *overdoers*, so called because they are "so busy doing things that there is no time to assess their true value." They are so engrossed in telling other people what to do — both at home and at work — that there is scarcely a moment for them to relax. Then there is the *time nut*. "Not an easy person to live with," says Lakein; this person is capable of saving eleven seconds eating cereal!

A fourth notorious character is the woman who lives with no organized system for getting through the day, the week, or the year. I call her the *mañana woman*. She is easy to recognize by the fact that she lives from one crisis to another. She never quite settles down to make lists, organize her day, or give any real thought to the direction of her life.

One woman shares her perception of time management this way: "Balance is important to any business owner. Have a system by which you are able to take time away from the business, participate in professional development programs, and know and practise the best way of stress management for you. Make time for yourself."

Self-Assessment

As an exercise, take a few minutes to think about your life and the relative importance of your business to the rest of it. To begin, make a list of your personal activities under the headings: *Willing to Give Up*, *Can Give Up*, and *Cannot Give Up*. Which of your activities are you willing to give up, can you give up, and which can you simply not give up? For those you feel you cannot give up, you might try combining one activity with another. For example, one business owner I know takes her ten-year-old daughter to horseback riding lessons every Saturday morning—without fail — and schedules appointments with potential clients near the riding school. That way, her daughter never misses the lesson, and she herself is free from motherly guilt. A woman who feels confident that she has made the best choices for her family works with even more vigour.

How and why we go about spending our time is primarily based on habit, other people's expectations, spontaneity, and conscious decision making. That process is called prioritizing. Before you are able to prioritize, you must first be aware of all the activities that go into making up your day. Below are two questionnaires to provide some insight into how you are spending your time, both at home and at work. For those of you who are currently not working in a business of your own, it may be challenging and fun to project yourself in the situation of an entrepreneur. There is no scoring for either quiz. At the end of each, however, I have provided a guideline for positive and productive time management.

HOW I HANDLE MY TIME DURING BUSINESS HOURS

1. Do you feel you have control of your time?
   Sometimes __________ Most of the time __________ Never __________
2. Do you try to plan ahead for:
   Each week? Sometimes __________ Most of the time __________ Never __________
   Each month? Sometimes __________ Most of the time __________ Never __________
3. Do you have a To-Do list and assign the activities a priority rating?
   Yes __________ No __________
4. Can you estimate how long each task should take?
   Usually __________ Never __________

5. Are you aware of how long you actually spend at each task?
   Yes __________ No __________
6. Do you allow for ample lead time as well as for last-minute adjustments?
   Never think about it __________ It would be impossible __________ Never __________
7. Do you usually pick the easiest or most pleasant tasks to do first?
   Yes __________ No __________
8. Do you allow yourself to delegate a substantial portion of your work to employees?
   Yes __________ No __________
9. Have you considered the possibility that you should be delegating more?
   Yes. It would be impossible to do. __________
   Yes. I would rather do it myself and make sure it is right. __________
   No. I do not have time to explain or supervise. __________
10. Do your employees show initiative and a keen interest in your business?
    Sometimes __________ Usually __________ Never __________
11. What is the average length of time you spend on the telephone with:

with:	5 min. or less	15 min. or over	over ½ hour
friends:			
clients:			
staff:			

12. How long does it take you to make decisions on simple matters?
    Instantly __________ Mull it over a few days __________
    Never can decide __________ Get someone else to decide __________
13. How long does it take you to make decisions on complex matters?
    Instantly __________ Mull it over a few days __________
    Never can decide __________ Get someone else to decide __________
14. How much time each day do you spend on routine tasks?
    15 minutes __________ More than one hour daily __________ Half the day __________

15. When you delegate a task or function to your employees:
    Do you check it regularly? Yes __________ No __________
    Do you let them solve their own problems?
    Yes __________ No __________
    Do you do the job yourself before they have a chance to get to it?
    Generally __________ Sometimes __________ Never __________
16. How much of your working day is spent on non-business activities such as clubs, associations, or social matters?
    A couple of hours a week __________
    A morning a week __________
    Part of every day __________
17. Do you take time in your working day to run personal errands — taking clothes to cleaners, getting shoes repaired, getting nails manicured?
    Never __________ When the workload is light __________
    Why shouldn't I? It is my privilege as the boss __________

What insight have you been able to gain? Is this the first time you have tried to evaluate your own time management? If it is the first time, can you figure out why you have been avoiding it?

Whether it is a To-Do list or another type of priority rating system, you must control your time, rather than let time control you. It is essential that you be able to at least guestimate how much time any particular activity should or will take. Try to become more aware of time. You may be kidding yourself about "free" time and simply wasting time. Learn to be aware of the frequency of the feeling that there is never enough time. Allowing time for last-minute adjustments will greatly ease your anxiety level and encourage more precision in your work. Doing the most pleasant tasks first is a good way to ensure failure.

If you are spending over five minutes on the telephone with friends, meet them for lunch instead. Some people select a particular time during the day when they return all personal calls; some wait till evening. The point is, if one of your employees played Chatty Cathy on the phone several times a day, how long would she be on your payroll? An appointment with a client can be set up in a matter of minutes. If you are serious about wanting their business, pay a trip to their office or invite them to yours. Who knows, you may even get them to make a commitment in writing, which of course is impossible over the telephone.

Beyond acknowledging the beautiful weather and other communication necessary to show you are human, your communication with your staff should serve a purpose. Did you recently get a new piece of equipment installed? Go and talk to the operator to see how it is working out. Show you care and are interested in their welfare without making them your best buddy. Hands-on management is what excellence in any company is all about today. Make sure you are communicating your expectations and listening to theirs. Some of the best corporate ideas come from employees who don't even know what colour the president's chair is.

Simple decisions should be made immediately. Complex ones may need some consultation with others. The ability to recognize when and if you are out of your field of expertise is the mark of a realist. You may find yourself underqualified in some areas or just plain overworked. Decide which it is and be willing to do something about it.

Take a look at your ability to let go of tasks. It is not surprising that women have problems delegating. According to Margaret Hennig and Anne Jardim in *The Managerial Woman*, most women's managerial style does not encourage initiative, or lend itself easily to delegating responsibility. It sends a very clear message — the boss trusts and relies on herself alone. Delegation has been called both an art and a science. The science of delegation lies in knowing how much to turn over to someone. The art of delegation lies in selecting the right person for the job. New entrepreneurs often feel that by delegating they are losing control over their business. But the more you are able to make constructive use of others, the more flexibility you acquire, and the closer you come to your goals.

Your working day, regardless of whether or not you are actually in the office or in the plant or wherever your normal business days are spent, should be used for business-related activities. A Business Executives meeting at 7:00 in the morning is a great way to start the day. Be aware of whether the meeting drags on until 10:00, with coffee and non-business-producing conversation. If hearing a speaker at lunch will inform you, or add to your growth as a person, by all means, go for it — take two and a half hours. Better still, you be the speaker! But not *every* day.

Watch those personal errands. If you're finding your workload a little light one day, shame on you — you're not working hard enough. Don't be surprised if it keeps getting lighter — light enough to put you out of business. Use this time to your advantage. Remember, in any business, time is money. If you're not making it, you're losing it.

Now, let's look at your private life.

HOW I HANDLE MY TIME AT HOME

1. I take a minimum of one hour for myself every day.
   Always ________ Sometimes ________ Never ________
2. I feel unsettled when things in the house remain undone so I push myself to make sure things are always clean and tidy.
   Always ________ Sometimes ________ Never ________
3. I make sure that my children get every form of activity they request regardless of how exhausted or short of money I am.
   Always ________ Sometimes ________ Never ________
4. When my husband is home I feel comfortable asking him to do specific tasks to help me around the home.
   Always ________ Sometimes ________ Never ________
5. My children are of an age when they can be increasingly more responsible for themselves. I encourage them to do so.
   Always ________ Sometimes ________ Never ________
6. Even though my business is taking considerable investment, I have arranged a housekeeper once a week to do general cleaning.
   I cannot afford it, but I do it. __________
   I am considering it. __________
   I need to do it myself. __________
7. I take time daily to communicate directly with my children that my business is very important to me and that I need their cooperation.
   They wouldn't understand. __________

I have their support. __________
I don't want to involve them. __________

8. When I am very stressed, I drop whatever I am doing as soon as possible and utilize my favourite stressbuster (e.g., tennis, walking, aerobics, yoga).
Always __________ Sometimes __________
I've got to be freaking out first. __________
9. I am sure that my priorities must be arranged now that I have my own business.
I have proof. __________
I have not noticed any need to change. __________
I am aware of it and am working on it. __________
10. I am able to express openly and honestly to my mate and friends that I am unable to spend the quantity of time with them I used to. When I do this I feel:
Like I am betraying them. __________
Proud that I am able to be assertive. __________

Again, ask yourself, now that you have gone through this exercise, what insight you have been able to gain into yourself. For most women the hours they put into homecare and nurturing are so much a part of role expectations that time is not always a consideration. But women who choose to go into business for themselves come to the reality rather abruptly: time acquires a whole new meaning. Taking time for yourself becomes more important than ever. I know of one woman entrepreneur who locks herself in the bathroom away from her family, responsibilities, and pressures, to be soothed by the sparkles and softness of giant bubbles in her daily bubble bath.

If you have ever suspected that you may be trying to be a superwoman, now is the time for re-assessment. The need to ask for help, and to break old patterns, has been realized by many women in business. In the words of Megan Abbott, the editor and publisher of Canada's only regional women's magazine, *Woman to Woman*, "I had to rebuild family relationships during the start-up period." Although she had been in business with her husband for years, owning her own enterprise caused a lot of changes, enough to seek professional help. Some of you will have already determined that whatever the price of success, for you, it is worth it. Having determined this, get ready for some serious juggling acts.

The Five-Step Plan of Attack

This program consists of carefully and methodically noting exactly how you spend your time during the day, both at home and at work. It will help you to prioritize. You will need two pieces of paper and a few sharp pencils.

Step 1 — Make two lists, each representing a 24-hour day. Top one sheet of paper with each of the following headings:

A Things I Must Do at Work

B Things I Must Do at Home

Now start writing, making use of both lists at the same time. Do not judge or edit your decision-making process at this time — simply keep listing activities at random. This is sometimes called brainstorming. Some women will end up with five items on each list, while others like Suzanne Fennell have fifteen to twenty. But the information given, or the size of the lists, is not the issue. The point is simply for you to be aware of how much you are trying to squish into your 24-hour day.

Step 2 — Give yourself a break. Smell a rose, have a cup of coffee, hug your baby, pat your dog. Do something to divert your attention from the lists for about fifteen minutes. When you feel you have sufficiently divorced yourself from the compulsion to keep adding, your lists are probably complete.

Step 3 — When the lists are no longer fresh in your mind, go back to them and delete from each list 10 per cent of what you have written down. For example, if List A has ten items — pay office rent, order supplies, negotiate new lease, start on bank proposal, get chair repaired, return phone calls, hire assistant, place ad in paper, train new employee, order lunch — delete one (probably "get chair repaired"). The 10 per cent cut should consist of things that can be put off without dire consequences for your business.

Now do the same for List B. As you can see, the woman who owns a business is in fact running two businesses — her household as well as the business the world gets to see. Now that you have listed your activities and have taken off your 10 per cent, it is time for Step 4.

Step 4 — Rank your activities according to priorities. Use *High, Medium,* and *Low*, or *A, B,* and *C.* It does not matter how you identify the activities which are urgent, those which should be done, and those which can wait. What does matter is that you use the same system of coding for both your business and your personal life. A word of caution: according to Lakein, most *A* or high priority activities will probably never get done the first time they are listed. "The problems associated with them," says Lakein, "are new, untried, unknown, and uncertain. Doing them means taking risks, which, whether calculated or not, will sometimes bring on unsuccessful outcome. An A . . . may appear to be of overwhelming complexity, or too time-consuming, or require reconciling views of people who can't or won't agree."

No wonder most of us piddle around with *B*s and *C*s. Have you ever realized that in the course of a day you found time to do everything except those things which were really important? I know of one designer who worked out of her home. She lived alone and had a room specially designated as her business room. She would wander around the house doing activities that had absolutely nothing to do with earning a living. So if you are trying to take a realistic look at your time management, be honest by acknowledging that lots of *C*s are make-work, *B*s are the day-to-day operations, and *A*s, although sometimes intimidating or just plain unpleasant, may affect the long-term success or failure of your enterprise.

Lakein has engineered what he calls his 80/20 rule. It goes like this. "If all items are arranged in order of value, 80 per cent of the value would come from only 20 per cent of the items, while the remaining 20 per cent of the value would come from 80 per cent of the items." With this in mind, go on to *Step 5*. Rank your *High, Medium*, and *Low* again by ranking them in *numerical* order of importance. Delete from your list another 20 per cent you suspect will not get done anyway. To make it easy on yourself, eliminate one item that you feel will be difficult, and one which gives you no particular anxiety. Let's take a look at what your new list might look like.

A List H pay office rent
L (order supplies) secondary 20 per cent
M negotiate new lease

H start on bank proposal
L (get chair repaired) original 10 per cent
M return phone calls
H hire assistant
M place ad in paper
L (train new employee) secondary 20 per cent
M order lunch

The secondary 20 per cent cut took ordering supplies off the list. If you are going to hire an assistant, ordering supplies is a good way to break her in. As for training the new employee, delegate that job to someone else once the assistant has been hired. So out of the ten necessary daily work activities, there are really only seven (six if you exclude a business lunch and make it a fun time rather than work).

The remaining seven items need to be ranked in order of priority numerically. If this were my office, I would definitely start off by paying the rent. Starting on a bank proposal for a sizable loan may cause anxiety, but it needs to be faced; your business could depend on it. Assuming you are expanding and can afford it, hiring an assistant is a high priority, since the more you can delegate, the more you can generate new business. Although negotiating a new lease is essential to remain in your present facilities, you do have two months before yours runs out. In the meantime, you may want to do a little comparison shopping. Returning phone calls is essential to the efficient operation of your business. Pick one time during the day and do them all at once. There are two reasons: one is that you will likely be less inclined to talk as long because of the volume of calls to be returned, and two, grouping all the calls together helps to keep you less scattered and more focussed. The ad you want to place in the paper can be taken care of by your new assistant. Again, learn to delegate.

The last, medium priority is lunch. Some people would never put this on their list. I insist, because skipping lunch is unproductive from an energy standpoint. Not only that, the mind needs restorative time and nutrients for optimum performance. Be good to yourself.

With this sorted out, use the following guide as your Daily Activity Sheet. Note that the activity sheet asks you to claim your responsibilities — in other words, putting your name on that piece of paper is a way of consciously owning up to the tasks. Three-hole-punch your sheets and keep them in a binder. As the days, weeks, and months progress, you will be able to see first-hand your growth and ability to have more control over your time. Note at the bottom of the page a place for items not accomplished that day. Be sure to write them in and note what their priority level is. Are you consistently putting off high priorities? Use this sheet as a personal watchdog.

DAILY ACTIVITY SHEET EXAMPLE

Name: Anne Demko Date: September 10, 1987

Activity	Priority Level	Comments
pay office rent	H-1	completed
start on bank proposal	H-2	phoned bank manager for appointment started working on first draft of proposal
hire assistant	H-3	hired Deborah, to start tomorrow
return phone calls	M-1	half returned
order lunch	M-2	completed, took short walk
place ad in paper	M-2	delegated to Deborah
negotiate new lease	M-3	tabled to have Deborah start comparing prices next week
get chair repaired	L-1	did not get around to it yet

Not accomplished today:

1. get chair repaired	Priority: L-1
2.	Priority:
3.	Priority:

What time management really amounts to is finding a solution for the problem of time not used well. Time management is a learned skill. At the beginning, you may feel that it is taking more time to figure out how to use your time than to do the activities, but the process will soon become second nature. Heather Cullimore and Valerie Muravsky, business partners in a Toronto dress design venture called Gladrags, put their challenge this way: "Business became an obsession. It was really bad. The business controlled us. We got burned out and started hiring people." One of the people they hired was Heather's husband. He not only helps with production, but is also househusband for the partners' three children.

Chapter 3

GOAL-SETTING FOR THE SERIOUS

I'm always getting back to the vision. I constantly have to remember that my message is for people to get fit.

Barbara Crompton, Founder, The Fitness Group Inc.

The Fitness Group is the leader in the fitness market in North America. It has a lot to do with Crompton's vision, her mission, and her goals. Here's how it works. Crompton's mission is to teach people fitness and healthy lifestyles; her vision was originally that people who normally did not like to exercise would learn to enjoy it in a safe, supportive, trusting environment. The goals that she has created in support of her mission and vision started with six to eight months of homework, complete with a small scale market analysis of who was out there teaching fitness and how.

Let's take a little closer look at mission, vision, and goals. Dr. Charles Garfield, a well-known American lecturer on high-performance achievers, talks about his early days with the NASA space project, when the late president John F. Kennedy had a mission — to put an American on the moon. You can be certain of one thing. Had Kennedy never had a vision (a vivid mental picture) of people in space, the mission would never have happened. The more I read, hear, and think about vision, mission, and goals, the more I am convinced that without a vision, goal-setting alone is basically a prescription for a life without purpose. The recipe for success is to Know the Mission, See the Vision, Activate the Goals.

Know the Mission

For a goal to qualify as a goal it must have a number of elements. It must be realistic, be relevant, have a plan of action, a method of rating success, completion date, and a system of rewards. One thing to keep in mind is that people who attain goals are no brighter, no more capable, nor more blessed than you or I. What they possess is dogged determination, backed up by a logical system for goal attainment. The key, then, is in the attainment of daily, weekly, monthly, and yearly goals as part of your day-to-day activities. For Barbara Crompton the goal-setting was well documented. It went something like this.

The goal had to be *realistic*. As an ex-teacher, she took control of the frustration aroused when she saw people who either did not like to exercise, or found it awkward, by asking herself, "How can I offer constructive advice and help so that these people too can have and enjoy fitness?" Her vision was fitness for all. She had spent a number of years in the advertising business, and had in earlier years been in budgeting for a company. But the most important asset she brought to her vision was her own high level of personal energy. Along with that came a conviction that people should be fit, as well as enthusiasm for her vision, love of herself, and a perception that the timing for a quality fitness program was good. Her original goal was "to have the best-developed fitness class in the Vancouver area and feel proud of it," says Crompton of those 1978 dreams.

The goal had to be *relevant*. While she had no one-on-one mentor, she was a devotee of Jane Fonda; through her, she saw the impact fitness could make in the business world. Says Crompton, "While I might not agree with all of Fonda's techniques, she has done a lot for the advancement of fitness and should continue to be acknowledged for it." The history of the fitness revolution is not long. But recently, Crompton was voted Canadian representative to the newly-formed International Dance and Exercise Association. That appointment is important because it signals that fitness is no craze, no fad, and several rungs above swallowing goldfish. It is probably here to stay.

The goal had to have a *plan of action.* Her plan of action was to go exercise-program shopping. She read and took courses in nutrition, marketing, business management, and kinesiology, and saw how the competition handled fitness. What she was able to do was isolate successful components in such specifics as group interaction, reaction to music and the instructor, and demographics of the class (male/female, age group, levels of fitness). She came away with the realization that people love to socialize. Both the instructor and the instruction were of critical importance, as were "the smile on the women and the 'buns' on the men." There was not only a market for fitness, but one that could be broken down into segments such as start-fit, ski-fit, pregnant, aerobic-weight, body shaping. Her in-depth analysis of the market gave Crompton her plan of action.

It is Crompton's intuition and ability to diversify that keeps her ahead of the pack. She has convinced corporate Canada as well as the provincial and federal governments that fitness translates into less employee absenteeism and bigger profits. "It was important that I establish myself as a leader for the quality of work that I do,'' Crompton says.

A *method of rating success* for Crompton was not necessarily determined by the bottom line on the balance sheet. Five to six thousand people a week take classes in her 4th Avenue, converted garage. They are led by a team of thirty-eight instructors. Probably another thousand are clued into stress management, fitness, and nutritional well-being through the University of British Columbia and corporate programs she has put in place. Is this success? Does she want to be city-hopping from one end of the country to another while her husband (who spends 40 per cent of his time devoted to the company) and three small children are at home? The questions remain, ''Is the biggest necessarily the best?'' Would two hundred people a week, in thirty small centres across Canada, do any more for her vision than what she has currently? To her, success is measured by the effectiveness of a one-city operation in turning a healthy profit and turning out a healthy clientele.

She did have a *completion date*. About three years ago she dreamed of going bigger, with higher numbers, more facilities. ''I got stumped with numbers. I had to get back to my vision. I am always getting back to my vision. I constantly have to remember that my message is for people to get fit.''

A system of *rewards*? ''Teaching is my reward,'' quips Crompton. When challenged that she may be too ethereal, she says, ''Every day I'm teaching something — a class or staff — something. I get so much back. My bottom line is to assist people on a daily level.'' She didn't want to talk dollars. I suspect there are plenty. She's entitled. She's innovative, hard working, committed to herself as well as her vision. Crompton's advice to other women going after this vision is, ''Forget being female. My being a woman is the most beneficial thing that could have happened to me.'' She's come a long way from the days when one of her primary goals was ''not to faint on the spot when leading a class.'' Today she doesn't faint; people listen — in the exercise arena or in the corporate arena. Crompton knows fitness.

See the Vision

Now let's take a look at where you are. Here's an exercise. Take a large sheet of paper and a pencil. You will be making a list. Start listing your goals both immediate and future, business and personal. Do not edit or question why you are writing what you do. Allow the spontaneity and creativity to flow. For example, your goals might read:

- to make a profit eight months after commencing business
- to spend three months of the year in a warm climate
- to have a loving and solid relationship with my partner

Most of us can come up with a dozen or so goals. Reaching the goals which lie beyond the dictates of logic or self-esteem at this stage in your life can require some work. I have devised a simple three-level exercise to help you get into better contact with your mission as well as your vision. I call it Levels in Support of Visionary Management. You can call it, "How in the heck am I going to get where I'm going?"

LEVEL I

1. Create goals for yourself. When everybody else is *thinking* goals, make sure you have yours. Know your mission. What is it you want to do more than anything else with your life? Barbara Crompton asks herself, "What do I want to do before I die?"
2. Create your own epitaph. Ask yourself what it is you have done in the world or would want to do that would make a difference. Spend a few minutes reflecting on your own sense of uniqueness, knowing that no other person is exactly like you; your position in history is unique. Acknowledge, explore, and develop this sense of self without fear of judgement, rejection, or recrimination. Go ahead, write your own epitaph. Begin with your name, date of birth (leave off death) but continue, "will be remembered for. . . . " Don't be shocked if you can't come up with one immediately.

LEVEL II

1. When everybody else is still out there *talking* goals, make sure you can see your vision clearly. What is it that you envision yourself doing or being in your lifetime?
2. Paint, write, or draw yourself doing and being exactly the

> person (you) who goes after and gets what she wants in life. This is a wonderful opportunity to make use of meditation. Some people are skilled at tapping into their dreams. They ask their subconscious for dreams that would depict themselves as successful and happy. If you have never tried it before, just before you go to sleep ask yourself (your subconscious) for a dream to expand your awareness of what you really want out of life. You may have to repeat the question five consecutive evenings. Your first thought upon waking should be the question asked again, so that you have recall on a conscious level. At this time you should get an answer.

You may want to try another process for expanding awareness. It is called visualization. In Shakti Gawain's *Creative Visualization* the process is explained. "In creative visualization you use your imagination to create a clear image of something you wish to manifest." I would like to admit here and now that I visualized myself right through the writing of this book — it works! A friend of mine, a psychologist, credits visualization with getting her through the rather onerous task of writing her master's thesis. Every day in her mind's eye or imagination she saw herself receiving her graduation diploma and visualized herself working with her clients as a practising psychologist.

Gawain says that the universe is made up of energy and that what we are is what we create. Peter Pocklington put it nicely when he said, "What we think, we become." What it means is that whenever you have a thought like, "I will create a rewarding business for myself," the positive thought energy gets transferred into energy of action, and *voilà* a rewarding business is created. Gawain says that, "a thought or idea always precedes manifestation. 'I think I'll make dinner,' is the idea that precedes creation of a meal." Yours may be, "I want a successful business." This thought is necessary before any level of success can be expected. Use your imagination; you've been playing with it all your life. Now is the time to put it to work. Go ahead and create in your mind whatever level of success you want. Fantasize as you did when you were a child, but believe in it as an adult.

LEVEL III

1. This is a very simple exercise in visualization. Start out by sitting quietly in a straight-back chair, both feet planted firmly on the floor, with hands resting on your lap, and simply close your eyes. Just be there and allow your thoughts to float freely. Try it every day for a week, for about five minutes at a time, and see if you can start to develop a sense of how you would like to be more of whoever you already are. Remember that imagination is a childlike gift we all have. Some people call it fantasy, others call it dreaming. Whatever you call it, understand that if you have the ability to visualize it, you have the ability to actualize it. Whatever it is you want — see it from the inside out and it is yours. And in Shakti Gawain's own words, at the end of every sitting say to yourself, "This, or something better, now manifests for me in totally satisfying and harmonious ways, for the highest good of all concerned."

Activate the Goals

Remember all those people out there simply *making goals*? When you know your mission and see your vision, goal-setting becomes nothing more than your guide to accomplishment. To illustrate with another story of success, the following chart shows how the business of Camelion Hosiery (Ross Hosiery Inc.) took form, from a fantasy to a million-plus, after only two years in business. What was fascinating to me was that Joy and Alaura Ross had done exactly what I am advocating, without our mutual knowledge of each other's philosophy. I prepared this list based on information provided by them.

LEVELS OF SUPPORT IN VISIONARY MANAGEMENT

Know the Mission

Mission: To be the Mary Kay of the fashion hosiery industry.

See the Vision

Vision: To have a good sales force of individual consultants all across Canada and the United States with each consultant building a loyal following.

Activate the Goals

1. They made a joint decision to live out a childhood dream of going into business together.
2. They considered several businesses, researched, and decided on hosiery.
3. They defined the business entity, goals, and philosophy.
4. They found a manufacturer for the product and a hired skeleton staff.
5. They engaged independent sales representatives to sell product.
6. They moved to a warehouse/clothing district to accommodate increased product volume and lines to be close to the fashion community.
7. They computerized, and they expanded staff, delegating whenever possible.
8. They expanded market into the U.S. and into eastern Canada. Vice-president and president exchanged roles and duties.
9. Priorities were now placed on recruitment of more sales representatives — currently at 300 to 400.

This company is interesting because the company goals were designed in unison. According to the Harvard Business School, goals are most effective when worked in unison — with a partner, a spouse, an associate. One associate of mine tells the story of attending a class at Harvard on goal-setting in which there were eleven participants. When asked of their goal one year from now, eight wanted new Lincoln Continentals (apparently the big, hot car at the time). The remaining three aspired to loftier goals. After one year, you guessed it, all eight got their Lincolns, and the other three achieved goals of considerably higher monetary and career value. The moral of this tale is, be careful what you ask for; you may get it. Which reminds me of a friend of mine who kept wishing for a silver-haired male in her life. The closest she came to getting her wish was a silver-haired stray male pussycat. Both are true stories. Be specific and be sure you really want what you ask for.

Back to the story of Joy and Alaura Ross. It is a fact that it had been their childhood dream to go into business with each other.

The career paths they took make them ideal business partners from the standpoint of complementing skills. While Alaura spent some time in banking, and secured a degree in economics before being called to the British Columbia bar, Joy was a top producer for Mary Kay Cosmetics. What they were able to package was a combination of hard business skills with sales and interpersonal skills — all essential for the type of business they were to create. While they had explored a few possibilities, the option they chose (maybe because Joy is the more aggressive of the two) was a company that would manufacture a non-run pantyhose. None of this basic, ''ick brown stuff'' — their products would appear in over a dozen fashion colours, and be as sheer as any medium-priced product on the market. Anyone with a little extra height can identify with Joy's need for a pantyhose that was capable ''of rising to the occasion.'' At five feet, nine inches, it was one frustrating pantyhose purchase after another. So a dream became a mission, a mission found a vision, and the goals were activated and, I expect, will continue to grow.

There are a number of products on the market in addition to Camelion Hosiery that are marketed through independent sales representatives. If there is any doubt in your mind as to your ability to conduct a business on your own, being an independent sales representative gives you the security of a corporate name behind you. People who sell real estate and insurance are, in fact, in business for themselves, but have the corporate identification of a larger body to back them with sales training, motivation, corporate logo, and maybe company benefits. Companies such as Mary Kay, Avon, gift and partywear companies, companies offering leisure-wear, and myriad others, are available and can be used as a stepping stone on the way to total independence.

In the case of Camelion Hosiery, their corporate role model is Mary Kay, while in the case of Molly Maid, McDonald's sets the example. It will be interesting to see how many other successful entrepreneurs choose not to re-invent the wheel, but simply learn from the best and modify the rest. Another point about Camelion is that their move to larger and more convenient premises in a more appropriate part of the city was the key to their growth. While it may not be necessary in your business to have flashy quarters to impress a client or potential employee, it is necessary to display a safe, comfortable, well-organized facility. In Camelion's case it was the right move.

But not everyone reports success. One woman claims, "In 1982 I tried to expand very rapidly. This proved to be a mistake because my income wasn't adequate to meet expenses. Although I didn't have to get a loan during this period, the expansion used up all my spare (working) capital. It took about eighteen months to get the business on an even footing again, even though I had gone back and reduced the size of it."

A prosperous modeling agency in Winnipeg met an even more crushing fate when the decision to expand led to its demise. Touch of Flare Agency was doing just fine providing models for trade shows and conventions in the Winnipeg area. It began as a stroke of good luck—Janis McInnes started out managing the agency and wound up owning it for the princely sum of one dollar. What went wrong? Three things, says Janis. "I used all my working capital for improvements. I expanded much too soon and at too great of an expense. I succumbed to the supermom syndrome. And the fact that I was a single mother was simply too tiring." A rule of thumb when it comes to expansion is very simple. What would expanding your business do to your profit picture in a given period of time? What would it cost you, and how soon could you recoup the investment?

Eight Steps to Success

There is yet another important exercise in goal-setting. It involves an eight-step process for walking yourself through to completion. But first, two areas need your attention. Procrastination is one. For all of us, even with the best and most exciting dreams and aspirations, visions and missions, we are all beset from time to time by that very dirty word. Procrastination is for most people simply an overextended period of fear. It is a form of avoidance behaviour, and the stress it creates speaks for itself. We all have fears: fear of the unknown, of failure, success, being wrong, getting angry, feeling guilty, being rejected, and in the case of entrepreneurship, it could well surface as a fear of too much responsibility. (It also frequently surfaces in parenting.) The next time you are aware of your own procrastination, ask yourself the question, "What is it I fear about this activity?" Then weigh the effects of the procrastination against the reality of what must be faced. Even a vivid "worst possible scenario" is usually less terrifying than the actual activity.

And secondly, since mission and vision can only be realized by the attainment of goals, you will need to start listing your goals and assigning a priority rating to them, just as you did in time management.

Take two blank pieces of notepaper and head one Long-Term Goals and the other Short-Term Goals. Keep in mind that "long-term" generally applies to goals spanning five years or more, while "short-term" is usually under. Some people even make use of a three-year time line. Whatever you choose, start listing the goals that will lead you to your mission, and rate them as in time management activities. For each goal make use of an Action Contract, as follows, and try to anticipate problems up the road. You may find you need to adjust some of your goals along the way. Some may not be physically, emotionally, or financially possible at the time. If this is the case, then find a solution and an acceptable alternative. While goal-setting may not solve all your problems on the way to a more successful life, it will be proof to yourself of your serious intent. The following Action Contract represents a step-by-step method for working your way through your goals one by one. You may want to adapt your Action Contract to suit your particular needs.

ACTION CONTRACT*

Date Commenced: __________ Date Completed: __________
This contract with (sign your own name)
________________________________ is in support of my mission, which is
____
____
because I can clearly see myself in (period of time)
____

*Adapted from Maurice Gibbons and Gary Phillips, "Self Education as a Deliberate Lifestyle: An Introduction to the Skills of Self-Directed Learning" (Simon Fraser University, Challenge Education Project, I.D.E.A., 1981)

____________________ doing/being ____________________
____
____.

This particular goal is: ______________________________
____.

It will allow me to move closer to my vision, and ultimately my mission.

STEP 1: Plan an outline of methods, activities, strategies, people, and resources you can use to help you attain your goal.
____
____
____
____

STEP 2: What do you perceive as the most difficult part of or challenge to acquiring this goal?
____
____
____
____

STEP 3: Anticipate problems that can go wrong. Take a look at possible obstacles, resistance from other people, your own personal shortcomings, and inclination to self-sabotage.
____
____
____
____

Strategies you are willing to employ to prevent problems:
____
____
____

STEP 4: You have a commencement date as well as a completion date. Now assign ''signpost'' dates so that you will accomplish segments of your goal.
1st date for accomplishment acknowledgement: ____
Task: ______________________________________
2nd date for accomplishment acknowledgement: ____
Task: ______________________________________
3rd date for accomplishment acknowledgement: ____

Task: ______________________________

STEP 5: Observe and note how you are performing to date. What needs to be improved or adjusted? (Rate your ability to stay on target.)

STEP 6: Observe and note how you are performing to date (generally).

____

____

____

NOW rate yourself as to your ability to remain on target for your goal.

On target _____ Wavering slightly but holding _____

Losing grip _________

STEP 7: Decide what is the minimum amount of growth or advancement toward your goal that you can

Live with: ______________________________

Feel comfortable with: ______________________________

Feel proud about: ______________________________

STEP 8: Create a circumstance where you will be in a position to let people know, or let them see for themselves, that you have successfully met your goal.

STEP 9: Self-reward. Make this dependent on the level of achievement you have been able to attain based on Step 6.

Greatest reward: ______________________________

Great reward: ______________________________

Nice reward: ______________________________

SUMMARY:

What self-knowledge were you able to obtain in monitoring your goal in this way?

____

____

____

Chapter 4

GETTING DOWN TO BUSINESS

Right at the beginning, start working out a plan for moral support.

Shelagh Lerand,
President, Proper Nails Inc.

Moral support, business support, and any other kind you can lay your hands on will be needed to see you through what most entrepreneurs consider the most difficult part of preparing to launch their dream. It's called the Business Plan. "In simple terms, a business plan is a down-to-earth assessment of how much money will be required, what the risks will be, and how much profit can realistically be expected to be made from the venture," according to the B.C. Innovation Office. They further advise that the plan must be based on facts, so be prepared to back up everything you say. It is the laborious and time-consuming fact-finding that most entrepreneurs feel takes all the fun out of starting a business. It may help to know that it's no fun failing, either. So do yourself a favour and go through the steps. You have everything to gain. Basically, the plan will provide you, the management, with some essential tools for growth as well as with assistance in evaluating your chances for success. If you're in the market for venture capital, even a small bank loan, the plan is essential so that future investors can evaluate their risk in your enterprise.

A friend of mine who is a director of a major Canadian venture capital fund shares the following observations: "Invariably, the investment opportunities we look at are the results of a brilliant mind from a narrow discipline. We see products and services presented by biologists, veterinarians, farmers, chemists, engineers, technicians, and so on. Almost without exception, investment in potentially great ideas is declined because they do not have a marketing plan. They all make the assumption that because they have been successful in their own discipline, and have found a better mousetrap, that the investors will beat a path to their door. In this competitive age, the world doesn't even know where their door is. And unless or until they surround themselves with people who have a clear understanding of the marketing process, the chances of their being successful are virtually zero."

Let's not deceive ourselves. Banks are not in the risk business — they want security. Venture capitalists are in the risk business; they're less interested in security. They want a piece of the action. It works like this. When you pay a bank loan off, you own 100 per cent of your business. If you bring venture capitalists in to provide the money, they will be 10 per cent to 30 per cent — or more — partners for life! The more money they put up, and the higher the risk, the bigger piece of the company they are going to want. While a decision to invest is rarely made solely on the strength of the business plan, the decision not to invest may be made based on its weakness.

According to the B.C. Innovation Office, the business plan should contain all the important critical factors involved in the venture:

1. The management team.
2. The money-making opportunities for the proposed business venture.
3. The development (or engineering) of the product (or service).
4. The manufacture of the product (or implementation of the service or establishment of the retail outlet).
5. The sales and distribution.
6. Financing the venture.
7. Operating the business.

You may be able to omit items 1, 6, and 7 if you are planning to license your product. If you are a manufacturer or an inventor, you should indicate the protection of proprietary interest.

Keep in mind that the business plan must be presented in an easy-to-read, simple format. Whenever possible avoid technical terms and trade jargon. If they are impossible to avoid, a simple explanation of the terms at the beginning may be useful to some readers.

Spending money on having your plan professionally prepared is a sensible investment. While the business concept may be your idea, few entrepreneurs are in a position to put together a cohesive plan by themselves. A good business consultant should be in a position to help you with this.

Before You Start

Let's carry that a step farther. In *Entrepreneurship: A Primer for Canadians,* William E. Jennings suggests that an effective business plan will assess three critical elements: 1. the entrepreneur's own capabilities and limitations; 2. market characteristics such as the market niche the firm would fill, the physical plant requirements, and the profit picture; and 3. the required human, technical, and economic resources. There are thirteen suggested steps to take in developing your business plan, according to Jennings.

1. Decide to go into business for yourself.
2. Analyze your strengths and weaknesses, paying special attention to your business education and desires. Then answer this question:
   Why should I be in business for myself?
3. Choose the product or service that best fits your strengths and desires. Then answer these questions: What is unique about my product or service? How do I know it is unique? What will my product or service do for customers? What will it not do? What should it do later but does not now do?
4. Research the market for your product or service to find answers to such questions as these:
   Who are my customers? Where are they? What is their average income? How do they buy? At what price? In what quantities? When do they buy? When will they use my product or service? Where will they use it? Why will they buy it? Who are my competitors? Where are they? How strong are they? What is the total market potential? Is it growing?
5. Forecast your share of market if possible. Then forecast your sales revenues over a three-year period, broken down as follows:
   First year — monthly
   Second year — quarterly
   Third year — yearly
   Next, answer this question:
   Why do I believe my sales-revenue forecast is realistic?
6. Choose a site for your business, then answer this question:
   Why do I prefer this site to other possible sites?
7. Develop your production plan, answering questions such as:
   How big should my facility be?
   How should my production process be laid out?
   What equipment will I need? In what size?
   How will I control the waste, quality, and inventory of my product?

(Obviously, these questions are slightly different for a service or retail business).

8. Develop your marketing plan, answering such questions as these:
   How am I going to create customers? At what price? By what kinds of advertising and sales promotion? Through personal selling? Direct mail? How?
9. Develop your personnel plan, answering this question: What kinds of talent will I need to make my business go? Draw up an organizational chart that spells out who has what authority, and who reports to whom. Authority and responsibility must always match.
10. Decide whether to form a sole proprietorship, a partnership, a corporation, or co-op.
11. Decide the kinds of records and reports you plan to have and how you will use them.
12. Develop your insurance plan, answering this question: What kinds of insurance will I need to protect my venture against possible loss from unforeseen events?
13. Develop your financial plan by preparing such statements as these:
    - A three-year cash budget, showing how much cash you will need before opening for business, and showing how much cash you expect will flow in and out of your business, broken down as follows:
      First year — monthly
      Second year — quarterly
      Third year — yearly
    - An income statement for the first year only.
    - Balance sheets for the beginning and ending of the first year.
    - A profitgraph, showing when you will begin to make a profit.

    Then determine how you will finance your business and where you expect to raise money.
14. Write a covering letter summarizing your business plan, stressing its purpose and its promise.

Writing Your Plan

Let's look at the plan step-by-step, as it is suggested by the B.C. Innovation Office. I have adapted their recommendations to suit an audience that is probably going to set up a retail or service business rather than a factory.

I *Title Page* (maximum one page)
The title page will be the cover page for the business plan and should contain:

1. The name of the product or title of the business venture.
2. The full legal name, address, and telephone number of the company or individual who is preparing the plan.
3. The date the plan was prepared (to be changed each time the plan is amended).
4. Name of the individual who can be contacted regarding the business plan. Also indicate your banker, lawyer, and accountant, including addresses and phone numbers.
5. A notice clearly stating that the business plan is confidential and is not to be divulged or released to any other parties without permission of the company.

II *Summary* (maximum one page)
Sometimes called the Executive Summary, it is prepared after the business plan has been put together. While it should be an inducement to read further, it should not be a repetition of what is contained in the actual business plan. Contents:

1. The purpose of the business plan.
2. A brief outline of the proposed business venture or product.
3. Highlights (main points only) of the reasons why the proposed business venture or product is considered to be a good investment or lucrative business opportunity.
4. Amount of financing and purpose(s) for the financing.
5. What you are prepared to offer in return for the financing.
6. A statement declaring that the business plan does not constitute a prospectus or public offering for financing and that no guarantees are made nor implied with regard to the success of the proposed venture.

Note: If your business is small, and you are approaching a lending institution for a loan in the area of five to ten thousand dollars, a statement of declaration is not necessary, unless you see many spin-offs for your business in the future, and there is a chance of an implied return somewhere up the road for the investor.

III *Table of Contents* (maximum one page)
Just what it says, and just as it appears on any document or book. It is an itemized list of main sections and subsections of the plan. List the titles or headings and the applicable page numbers.

IV *Introduction* (maximum two pages)
The introduction provides a brief history or background of the company, as well as the purpose of the business plan. It includes:

1. The reason or reasons for setting up a business plan. Whether it is to obtain financing, set up production, sell the product for commercialization, complete development, or arrange distribution, you must have a plan.
2. A brief overview of the proposed product or business venture.
3. A brief history or general background of the development of the idea or product up to the present time.
4. The amount of money required and the specific purpose for same.
5. A brief statement of the terms and/or conditions in the event the financing is successful (what you are prepared to offer in return for investment in your business).

V *The Company or Individual* (maximum one page)
The purpose of this section is to identify the company (or person) responsible for preparing and carrying out the plan. If the company is an individual, state your full legal name, address, and telephone number. Briefly state your qualifications and particular expertise related to your product or proposed business venture.

State when and where the company was (or will be) incorporated and include the company's full legal name, address, and telephone number. Include the main reasons the company was established or its intended primary area(s) of business activity. State the number of employees as well as the present company premises. You'll need to identify a contact person in the event someone wants to discuss the plan.

VI *The Management Team* (maximum two pages)
A prospective investor must have confidence in the management team. A strong team is considered critical to the approval of an investor. The investor must feel convinced that the key people have the ability to meet the objectives of the business plan. The team will consist of those who will be responsible for both executive as well as day-to-day management of operations. Your management team must have been selected prior to your business plan. Investors will want to know: their name, responsibilities in the new organization (job function), and a brief summary of the key qualifications and relevant experience. It's not a bad idea to have a resume of each team member available on request.

It may be that, due to conflict of interest or other reasons, a member does not want to be identified by name. In this case, state in a general way their current function as well as their proposed place on the team.

What is equally important to include is the number of shares (if any) key members currently own in the product or proposed venture.

In the case of many new ventures, you alone comprise the team. In this case, your education as well as relevant job experience will be an essential part of selling yourself. In the event that your past job experience is not relevant to the business you are creating, you'd better have at least one other team member who can satisfy a potential investor's need to know who will make the business successful. What might be useful would be to include a time frame for the addition of others to your business, particularly in areas in which you are weak. You may be able to justify certain absences by making use of consultants when needed.

VII *Other Shareholders* (maximum one-half page)
Identify any other shareholders or owners of the product or proposed venture along with the number of shares or percentage of ownership. Briefly explain the shareholders' relationship to the company. Are they active management? Are they prepared to sell their interest? It is important to be very specific.

VIII *The Product* (maximum two pages)
Avoid detailed descriptions. Provide a brief summary of what the

product is or what it does, its major features and benefits, the innovations and/or technological advantages inherent in the product, and application(s) or purpose(s) of the product. The summary should contain the name of the product with a brief description of what it does or how it is used, and the major applications of the product (focussing on its key qualities or particular strengths and advantages). Along with the important features and benefits and why it is so special, include a description of any innovative features, advanced technology, or unique design. Mention here, too, whether the product is currently patented or is intended to be, along with any legal rights you have exercised to protect the concept or idea. (Remember not to divulge any details that could jeopardize the protection of your product.)

IX *The Marketplace* (maximum two pages)
Here is the place for a brief summary of the major market(s) for the product. The primary emphasis should be on the size of the market that will account for the major sales of this product, why the product is required, and its distribution process. The marketplace must be described in specific terms. All information must be founded on good research that you are able to substantiate. Save all market survey and other support information for future reference.

In your information about the marketplace you must decide the geographical location(s) for the major market(s) — that is, whether your product will be marketed only in one city or in Canada, the U.S., the U.K., and so on. Include the total market potential or sales opportunities — the total number of potential buyers, as well as buyers of competitive products. Current or committed orders, as well as the number of sales of both similar or competitive products over the past two years, should also be included. State the expected growth of the market over the next five years (expected increase in product sales per year) and list the major users or potential customers.

If your product is for the consumer, describe the market in terms of how the consumer will use the product and why. Include, too, why anyone would buy the product. What is it hat makes it saleable or marketable? Let them know how the specific needs of the marketplace will be filled and how.

If your product is industrial or commercial, list the major users of the product by corporation name and whether or not these users will be large, well-known organizations. It is important that you take this one step further by summarizing, in one or two paragraphs, why the product will have wide market acceptance, and why in your opinion the venture will be commercially viable. Include what the market is prepared to pay for your product (end user or retail price). Describe the marketplace to enable the reader to get a better grasp of the consumers, and to be able to form an opinion of the market, as well as money-making opportunities. In addition, every effort should be made to obtain valid letters of intent, purchase orders, or whatever you consider would be proof of market acceptance. Name the sources of your market information, market surveys, and reports. Again, be careful when providing information that you do not give away too much.

X *The Competition* (maximum one page)
Your plan must be able to convince the reader that your product will sell successfully against the competition. You must identify the competition and competitive product(s) as they will likely impact on your sales. The page on competition should contain the names and locations of major competitors, along with the share of the market they currently enjoy. Included, too, should be the major features and benefits of each competitor's product along with selling prices. A comparison between theirs and yours is important; highlight the advantages of yours over the competition's. Include a brief description of the key strengths or major reasons for acceptance of your competitor's product (large distribution and service network, world-wide or across Canada, and so on). Being as factual as you can, describe any known weaknesses of your competition's product. Describe the distribution and sales approach used by your competition, along with any voids you feel your product can fill in the marketplace.

XI *Sales Plan* (maximum two pages)
In this section you must summarize your specific plans to explain how you are going to sell your product and penetrate your target market. This is your opportunity to address the type of sales organization you have put together, your advertising and

promotion, along with the sales methods and sales forecast. You must provide a brief summary of the methods you plan to use to sell (distribute) the product in the marketplace. Whether it is through direct sales (winding up as retail sales), through distributors or dealers (wholesale), mail order, or any other way, be specific.

Briefly describe the type of sales organization you are setting up to get the products into the marketplace (manufacturing agents, internal sales selling directly to the customer, through distributors or dealers, etc.). Describe the size of the internal sales organization required to sell the product, along with the number of sales people required and whether a branch is necessary. State the proposed methods of advertising and promotion (advertising in trade shows, periodicals, trade publications, etc.). Indicate your penetration process: will you start locally, then expand?

Provide a forecast of projected sales for the product over the next three years. Segregate the years into one, two, and three, and consider year one as the first after receiving financing. If your product is undergoing further development, or you know that more than a year's lead time is necessary for it to hit the market, then show year one as zero sales and extend the sales forecast to include at least three years from the time the product is ready for the market.

XII *Product Development* (maximum one page)
Keep in mind that this plan was originally devised for businesses going into manufacturing, where product research and development would occupy a lot of the pre-planning time and money. Regardless of your business, summarize the stage of development your product is currently enjoying, and the stages yet to be completed before your product or service is ready for the marketplace (distribution, utilization). Briefly describe the present status of development and what is required in terms of phasing by time (for example, two months, six months, one year). Try to be specific when anticipating any problem that may be impossible or difficult to solve along the way.

XIII *Production* (maximum one page)
In this section, give an outline of the general methods of, or approach to manufacturing, or of getting the product into the marketplace in terms of facilities and time needed. How will your

product or service actually be carried out — physical location, stages in bringing the product or service to the public (through promotion, advertising)? How will your work actually be done — manually, or by high-technology? Are you planning eventually to become unionized? Do you need to seek government approval for your physical location? Are you planning to do all the work yourself or will you be subcontracting? Is there any element of your business that may present a production problem (for example, only one source of paper for lithography)?

XIV *Product Cost and Gross Profit* (maximum one page)
The gross profit is the difference between the money you receive per unit or project, and the unit cost of production. For those in manufacturing, the product cost will be the total of the material costs, plus the direct labour costs (wages and fringe benefits) to assemble or manufacture the product. For those, for example, in a consulting business, your costs are your time billed plus any disbursements. Whether you pay yourself a regular monthly or weekly salary or compensate yourself on a percentage of your billings, you must know how much it costs you to run your business. (Please see cashflow section of this chapter.)

XV *Financial Requirements* (maximum one page)
Do not include detailed calculations or itemized expense lists. These are your working papers and need to be filed for future use. This section is a summary of how much money will be required to meet the objective of the business plan until the venture is self-sustaining (that is, when additional financing is no longer required).

This section should contain a list of the major areas of expense defined in each section of the business plan — sales/marketing, product development (engineering) and production, administration. This total will be the total amount of money that you will require to meet all of the objectives of the business plan. This section, for those who are not concerned with production or manufacturing, should include costs involved in getting your retail outlet, product, or service into the marketplace.

XVI *Pro Forma Income Statements* (maximum one page)
This is a future projection or forecast of the profit (or loss) over a specific period of time. You will probably need an accountant

to help you do it. Once a company has been established, this statement is generally prepared once a month and is an itemization of how much money was earned (revenue) and how much money was spent (expenses) to earn the revenue during the previous month. In the pro forma statement, all you can do is forecast your anticipated earnings and expenses each year, over a period of three years, after financing is in place. Do not include items generally falling under capital equipment; for example, typewriters, computers, and automobiles.

XVII *Cashflow Projections* (Future Cash Needs)
The cashflow projections are necessary for you to determine the amount of investment or financing you will need from investors. It is, in fact, the amount of money required until the venture can be self-sustaining. As in the Pro Forma Income Statements, cashflow projections must be made for a period of three years.

The cashflow is the actual amount of cash or money that is available to you at a specific time. You must have adequate cash to cover yourself (rent, salaries, commissions, suppliers) until the product is actually selling. Do not forget to include money payable to the bank if it has advanced you money for capital equipment. Either from a bank or elsewhere, you will need to find a means of obtaining the money to keep your company afloat until money starts to come in. If you receive more money than you spend, you will be in an enviable, positive cashflow situation. If you spend more than you receive, then the situation is called a negative cash position. Opposite is a model for your cashflow projection. Again, an accountant will help you with this.

When you are finished, carefully review your business plan and make sure it is based on sound information and good business judgement. Remember that regardless of your potential lender, the name of the game is the same — how will you be able to repay? All investors are interested in is their repayment, and they will judge the likelihood of that by your capacity and your intention. Your capacity as an operating company is straight mathematics based on sound assumptions. For example, if someone lends you $100,000 and the business only has the capacity of showing a $20,000 profit yearly for the first five years, chances are the investor will wait well into the sixth year before seeing any capital

CASHFLOW PROJECTION

	Period 1	Period 2	Period 3
Sales (product delivered and invoiced)			
Revenue (money received or cash in)			
Expenses (money spent or cash out)			
Opening balance (amount of money or cash on hand at the start of the period)			
Closing balance (amount of money or cash on hand or required at the end of the period)			
Closing balance (revenue plus opening balance minus expenses)			

return. In other words, in this instance you probably do not have the capacity to repay the investment within an acceptable time frame. On the other hand, if the investments have the capacity to generate a $200,000 profit in the first year, the investor sees clearly that you do have the capacity to repay him within a reasonable period of time.

All investors will ask you for a statement of intentions. If the necessary capacity is there, what priorities do you have in the distribution of profits? They will want to know — on paper — that their money comes out before you declare any dividends, or acquire any significant additional capital assets. They do not want you to spend $50,000 on a piece of real estate, a Mercedes convertible, or a vacation in Spain, before they get some or all of their money returned. Before they make a decision on how their money is going to go into the company, you must be able to satisfy them with an absolutely clear statement of how their money is going to come out of the profits.

Keep in mind that all business plans are based on assumptions. They are seldom supported by facts, since there is no track record on which to build. Everything is brand new. You must find every possible way to assure your potential investor that the assumptions you have made in the business plan are realistic — leaning to the conservative side. Depending on the product or service, assumptions may be affected by the weather, geography, interest rates, competition, kind of manufacturing, trends, scientific data — the list is endless. Look for ways to assure your investor that you have thought of everything that could go both right or wrong before you have settled on the figures for his or her consideration. If a business cannot be worked out on paper, you probably do not have one. Getting out the pencils and paper, and actually committing the project to dollars and cents, can be exciting if not sobering.

Cashflow

Cashflow is so critical to the survival of your business that 98 per cent of the women I interviewed for this book found their lack of business experience in this area worthy of mention. Whether the problem is created by an actual cash shortage, undercapitalization at the outset of the business, or poor cashflow management, it is prevalent in most businesses. Robert Cohen, president of the Cohen Group in Toronto and teacher at York University, wrote in *Small Business* magazine that you should start out by preparing cashflow statements based on *forecasted* cashflows. The statements should be monthly for the first year, twice a year for the second, then yearly from then on. Be sure to include *all* cash movement: accounting expenses, legal disbursements, withdrawals, advertising, rent, and so on. Try to negotiate with suppliers to lengthen terms of payment and with purchasers to pay promptly. It not only improves cashflow but also shortens the term needed for bridge financing. Be sure to keep track of how much cash you require, when you require it, and figure out when you can repay. Then, with your plan of attack in place, go after those friends, family, bankers, and potential creditors. Explain how much you require, how and when you will repay, and at what rate of interest. Find the money before you need it. Even if your cashflow looks fluid enough, always seek a source of immediate help to ward off a financial crunch that can emerge, seemingly, from out of nowhere. Update your statements regularly.

"After seven years it is still nerve-wracking," says Susan Whitney, owner of the Susan Whitney Gallery in Regina, Saskatchewan. Whitney's comment could come from any sector of the business arena. No one industry gets to lay claim to more cashflow headaches than another. So whether you are the owner of a gallery like Whitney, or a public relations agency or a shop, the problems connected with what comes in and what goes out are legendary. What is supposed to happen (now that we have learned the lessons of sky-high interest rates and the recession) is that you get your cash in as quickly as possible, pay it out as slowly as possible, and work it as hard as possible while it's still in your hands. According to William Annett, writing in *B.C. Business*, "cash management has become a latter-day religion for large and small companies alike." In a recent survey by three leading American universities, 61 per cent of the businesses polled considered cash management the prime source of recurrent problems.

You can encourage your receivable accounts to pay on time in a number of ways. You may offer a volume discount, a special membership, or a discount for paying in cash or in less time than your established terms (ten, thirty, sixty, or ninety days). Before you give anyone credit, ask yourself if it is necessary. It may not be if yours is a consulting firm, for example. Such operations often require a retainer. If your projects are relatively small, then credit is probably unnecessary. Should the account be in the range of even a few hundred dollars, get a retainer — a sizable one. Put in writing an agreement stating when and how the balance will be paid. I know of one woman who contracted to do a specific project for a very large corporation. She asked for and received a sizable retainer. However, because there was no time-frame stipulation, by the time the client wanted her to perform the task, she had changed the direction of her work and was no longer performing that type of task.

At the very least, draw up a Memorandum of Understanding when contracting work. Spell out the nature of the job, the amount of money, the retainer, and the start and completion dates. Have a signature line for your signature and your client's (make certain they have the power to contract). In other words, get it in writing.

All new entrepreneurs know the urgency attached to new business. Frequently, they are either too busy or not experienced enough to follow up on their own receivables. Collecting can be difficult and extremely time-consuming. It can also cost *you* money.

You can minimize the risk of bad debts in a number of ways. You may want to accept major credit cards, take advantage (for a fee) of a cheque verification service, or establish *regular billing* (where bills are sent out on a regular basis), *billing on time* (where the bill is sent as soon as the service or product is received), or *accelerated billing* (net thirty or ten days or even due upon receipt). Before granting credit, consider the size of the order and the potential for more, the status of the present account, the length of time the customer has been in business, and any special arrangements you have made with the customer. Monitor the payment trends of your customers; if you determine that they are either not in a position to pay or will not pay, you should start your collection procedures immediately.

There are a number of ways to collect. You may want to send out a reminder with an appropriate statement, or pick up the phone and ask for money in one of three ways: installment payment plan, post-dated cheques, or promissory note. There is also another way: a collection agency will handle the collection of the debt for a fee, usually from 25 per cent to 50 per cent. It is costly, but it is safe to say that at times something is better than nothing.

Do yourself a favour by initiating a system of bad-cheque control. Do not be too trusting, nor too embarrassed, to insist on proper identification, or too slipshod to bother, or too busy to train your staff. Beware of people who object to showing proper ID, of a cheque issued by an unknown company (particularly a cheque from out of town or one not printed on regular cheque safety paper), a second-party cheque, a cheque presented on a weekend or holiday when contacting a bank is impossible, or one from a client who wants to write it for more than the value of the goods or services.

Liisa Nichol, president of Pirjo-Liisa Fashions Ltd. of Winnipeg, a company selling manufacturers' leftover merchandise through both home fashion parties and retail stores, sells by cheque, cash, or credit card only. In addition to maintaining a healthy cashflow, she maintains a line of credit with her bank. It is safe to say that with her $2,000 investment in 1975, and the present sales volume in the $7-million range, her system must be working.

Keep in mind that unless you are paid in advance, you always run the risk of not being paid. Know your customers, and make sure they know what is expected. This can be aided by:

- making sure terms are clearly understood;
- making sure your customer can meet the terms;
- billing promptly;
- demonstrating that you expect prompt payment;
- maintaining dated accounts receivable;
- following up overdue accounts, and
- engaging a professional collector as soon as you identify a problem.

Basically, accounts receivable are based on collection periods of:

- 60 per cent of receivables collected in thirty days;
- 30 per cent of receivables collected in sixty days;
- 10 per cent of receivables collected in ninety days;

Accounts receivable aging should look something like this:

CUSTOMER	1-30 days	31-60 days	61-90 days	over 90 days	Total
J.T. Farm	$375.00	$ 85.00	$ –	$ –	$460.00
R.G. Corp.	$ –	$ –	$250.00	$250.00	$500.00
Flowers Inc.	$100.00	$310.00	$ –	$ –	$410.00

Talk with other people in business about how they handle cashflow problems. Or you may want to take the advice of one east-coast entrepreneur. ''Cashflow can become a problem if you don't have a large enough line of credit, particularly when the business is growing. When accounts become doubtful, I take the customer to Small Claims Court. To date I have had to write off about $400; without Small Claims Court it would have been about $2,000. I am careful about who gets credit from my company.''

Simple Cashflow Projections

Below is a model for cashflow projections. Be realistic. Underestimated expenses for most businesses can be spotted almost immediately by people who understand business.

1. *Start-Up Costs*

   Business licence, incorporation, or other mandatory fees $__________

   Professional start-up costs: lawyer, accountant $__________

Insurance $ ______
Equipment, furniture, and fixtures $ ______
Advertising and promotion for opening $ ______
Deposit with utility or phone company $ ______
Add 25 per cent to cover something you forgot or do not know about $ ______
TOTAL $ ______

2. *Monthly Overhead*

Rent $ ______
Salaries $ ______
Advertising and promotion $ ______
Supplies and stationery $ ______
Utilities $ ______
Telephone $ ______
Postage $ ______
Delivery $ ______
Add 25 per cent to cover the unexpected $ ______
TOTAL $ ______

3. *Receivables*

List your invoiced accounts here. If the total amount in item 2 is greater than that in item 3, you have a serious cashflow crunch. When you are just starting up, you will also have item 1 to add to your expenses.

Below is a simple cashflow worksheet.

SIMPLE CASHFLOW PROJECTION WORKSHEET

Sample Quarterly Summary of Actual Cashflow (A) versus Planned Projections (P)

	JANUARY		FEBRUARY		MARCH		APRIL	
CASH RECEIPTS	P	A	P	A	P	A	P	A
Cash sales								
Collection of accounts receivable								
Loans								
Other cash receipts								
Total Cash Receipts								

	JANUARY		FEBRUARY		MARCH		APRIL	
CASH DISBURSEMENTS	P	A	P	A	P	A	P	A
Purchase of materials or stock								
Purchase of fixed assets								
Advertising								
Management salaries								
Other salaries and wages								
Rent								
Repair and maintenance								
Legal and accounting								
Licences and taxes								
Insurance								
Telephone								
Utilities								
Vehicle expense and travel								
Other operating expenses								
Interest and bank charges								
Payment on loans/mortgages								
Income tax payments								
Other cash expenses								
Total Cash Disbursements								
CASH SURPLUS OR DEFICIT								
OPENING CASH BALANCE								
CLOSING CASH BALANCE								

Two Essential Documents

To determine the good news or bad news of your business, you will need two documents: a financial statement and a balance sheet. Under normal circumstances your company will produce a monthly financial statement. It will tell you how much money you took in, how much money you spent, and list by category the expenditures you made. You will know at the end of every month if your sales exceeded your costs and you had a profit, or if your costs exceeded your sales and you had a loss. It is like taking a patient's temperature — the figure you get is precise and dependable. An accumulation of monthly financial statements over the course of a year will lead to the development of a Balance Sheet. Basically, a balance sheet lists the assets and the liabilities of the company — with most of the figures coming from the monthly financial statements. The ultimate health of the company is determined by the balance sheet.

Financial Statement

Below is a simple profit-and-loss statement, sometimes called a statement of income. Keep in mind that business income from a non-incorporated business is classified as personal income to the owner and taxed at personal tax rates.

The ABC Company
Financial Statement for month ending January 31, 1988

Revenue: Sales	$ _____
Less Cost of Goods Sold	$ _____
Gross Profit	$ _____
Expenses (overhead)*:	
Salaries and benefits	$ _____
Interest and bank charges	$ _____
Insurance	$ _____
Deliveries	$ _____
Advertising	$ _____
Rent	$ _____
Telephone	$ _____
Utilities	$ _____
Repair and maintenance	$ _____
Vehicle operating expenses	$ _____
Total Expenses	$ _____
Net Income (before taxes and owner's draw)	$ _____

*If you have made an investment in unsold stock, whether manufactured or purchased wholesale, this should also be added to your list of expenses.

Your net income had better be on the positive side if you want to stay in business. If you cannot pay yourself a living wage and make a profit, you might as well get a job and put your money in the bank.

THE BALANCE SHEET

The ABC Company
Balance Sheet
December 31, 1987—December 31, 1988

ASSETS:	$ _____
Cash on hand	$ _____
Accounts receivable	$ _____
Invested share capital	$ _____
Goods manufactured (but not sold)	$ _____
Fixed assets (real estate, office furniture, and fixtures)	$ _____
Supplies	$ _____
Tax credits (if any)	$ _____
Total Assets	$ _____
LIABILITIES:	
Accounts payable	$ _____
Long-term loans	$ _____
Depreciation	$ _____
Tax liabilities (if any)	$ _____
Total Liabilities	$ _____

Someone who wants to know the health of the company can compare the assets with the liabilities and determine whether or not the company is liquid, saleable, needs more working capital, or is bankrupt.

How It Actually Works: A Case Study

Let's take a look at what happened to Proper Nails Inc., which was launched in Toronto in 1984 by Shelagh Lerand, former Avon representative and gold-mine corporation president. According to Lerand, "The original company was born out of the desire to create a better mousetrap (artificial fingernails that were safer, less expensive, easier to apply, and more beautiful than those the competition was offering)." In the three years since the company's inception, not only has Lerand's product line changed but the whole direction of the company has as well. Let's take a look at how she set up the business and what has happened to it since its inception.

Lerand's original intention was to provide a business opportunity for her daughter. But the focus changed as she became more aware of the market potential. Beset with personal health and marital problems when the scouting for the perfect business was underway, Lerand had problems that were enough, she says, "to make a woman bite her nails." The idea hit her like a thunderbolt. She claims, "Any idea that wakes you up in the middle of the night can't be wrong. Don't listen to anyone else. Not your husband, your boyfriend, your well-meaning friends. If you believe in what you are doing and can put yourself in the position of the buying public, you've got a winner."

Interestingly, Lise Watier, dubbed Montreal's cosmetics queen, is quoted in the Montreal *Gazette* as saying, "I survived because I didn't look at the competition." Watier, Canadian businesswoman of the year in 1986 and president of Lise Watier Cosmetiques Inc., with $15 million in sales last year, confided, "Everybody told me, 'You're crazy. The competition is so strong.'"

It seems Lerand and Watier are like-minded. To accomplish their ends, Watier "went like a horse with blinders," Lerand employed her "steam-roller technique."

Lerand knew her market was in volume. Contrary to the business objectives of many entrepreneurs, her goal was not to make money, per se; it was to get enough people so excited about selling her product that they would meet their personal monetary goals. She would be a winner in two ways: she would, through the efforts of others, meet her own goals and objectives, and she would provide a product and service that helped others feel productive and successful. The concept was not new, and she saw no reason to re-invent the wheel. She researched by talking to people — lots of people — at malls from Calgary to the east coast, and asked them what they did not like about the product they were currently buying and wearing. She hired her chemists and the formulation for the better product began.

She was well aware of some of the negative press acrylic nails had been receiving, so she first researched the solutions to these problems. She became aware of the length of time for application and touch-up (or replacement) — knowing that time is money in any service business. She investigated every aspect of potential competition, and tried to anticipate all difficulties, from the "unpleasant fumes" to the "constant, permanent covering of the fingernail which needed to be exposed to air and to be monitored regarding its condition." She researched her market to find what she felt was a better method and a superior product.

As president of Proper Nails, Lerand is chief executive officer and holds all the stock. She herself has the last word in all corporate decisions. While she has the support of fifteen staff (from chemists to shippers), and twenty-five subcontractors, the ultimate success or failure of the business rests on her shoulders.

Luckily for Lerand, she started with a partner who had a business degree from McGill. That advantage took a lot of guesswork out of her proposal research, documentation, and presentation. Find someone who can help you. Accuracy is important. What if you should secure financing based on your plan, only to discover six months later that you had not requested enough? In all probability, your lack of expertise would be viewed with a jaundiced eye, leaving you in a sink-or-swim position. Do not be bashful about sharing your ideas with people you can trust. If you must, pay an accountant or management consultant to help you work through this challenge. Here are a few forecasting tips:

Step 1

Make some basic assumptions based on your market research.
Your customer is: male, female, young, middle-aged, retired.
Your customer is: blue collar, white collar, professional.
Your customer is: low, middle, upper income.
Your customer will: purchase once, purchase repeatedly.

Step 2

Make use of all regional statistics. Do some serious fact-finding as to the frequency of use of your products in the household and the number of them per household.

Step 3

Know your competition and estimate how much of their business you can swing your way.

Lerand had investigated her product and knew it to be superior to the competition's. Not only did she feel it was safer for the nail, but it also took exactly three minutes to apply from start to finish. The short application time, coupled with an estimated annual upkeep for a set of ten of $100, compared favourably with the competition's estimated upkeep of $300 to $500 annually. Lerand knew enough about the market (products, competition) and women to know that what had to be sold was personal attention to the consumer.

Her marketing is geared to the woman who considers beauty within her budget and is seeking instant beauty results. That woman is prepared to spend between $25 to $100 per visit, and is either a "nail biter who can't grow them, or has a history of managing to lose them in rapid succession." After test-marketing in over thirty trade shows across Canada, she was convinced she had a winner.

Her initial entry into the beauty industry with Proper Nails has grown prodigiously in a scant three years. She is currently marketing not only nail replacements but also synthetic re-usable fingernails (product and application adhesive) and two additional product lines. One is skin care with a gauge for self-assessment and prescribed skin care. The other is makeup, including eye makeup designed for delicate and allergy-prone skin. All formulas are patented. The original business has grown from a twenty-five-square-foot, one-person operation producing $45,000 in the first year, to $1 million gross revenue, produced by 500 independent distributors in 1985.

While the good news was that Proper Nails was growing by leaps and bounds, the bad news was that the growth was simply too quick and Lerand was losing control. "In effect," she says, "the business was running me."

It is critical to recognize when this loss of control is happening in your business. Lerand's ability to act on this sudden and unexpected growth allowed her to retrench and ultimately led her into new sales directions and even greater growth. As the demands, opportunities, and product lines grew, so did her dreams about her company. Sales are already in place on four different levels: $50 provides the sales representative with a small supply of nail goods for retail sales, where the selling can be done from the home;

$1,000 includes fully certified training and $1,400 worth of stock; $7,000 buys a mini-salon franchise (a turn-key operation), including stock of cosmetics, skin-care products, nail goods, business cards and flyers, along with a plan on how to create business; finally, the big one, a franchise operation for $40,000 to $60,000, includes a turn-key mall location with all of the above, plus a bookkeeping system and vendor's permit.

Lerand planned to market as the "fast-food of skin care, fingernails, and makeup." Originally run from her home, the company now occupies a converted building, complete with offices and warehousing, training and franchising facilities. The opportunity for expansion is in the remainder of the building. Most fixed assets are leased or acquired through subcontracting. While costs of equipment, transportation, product containers, packaging, and warehousing keep soaring, she feels her goals of opening franchises in Australia and the U.S. are not far from realization. Her goals are being continuously refined, and her plans to increase sales across the board in the next five years by 10 to 20 per cent are well underway. Lerand is placing her priorities on franchising and building a solid capital base for the establishment of forty franchises within the next three years.

You can see how the need to create a business, based on an innovative idea, took Proper Nails Inc. of Toronto from a one-woman, one-kiosk, artificial fingernail operation to an extended line of skin-care and makeup products, quickly growing into franchises world-wide. This expansion and diversification will not be everyone's dream, but the logistics look very encouraging for franchise operations in general throughout the marketplace, expecially those that render personal service.

Chapter 5

TO MARKET, TO MARKET

You have to put your heart and soul into it.

Liisa Nichol, President,
Pirjo-Liisa Fashions Ltd.

Liisa Nichol, a Winnipeg mother of four children, started her business of buying manufacturers' leftover merchandise and reselling it at home fashion parties in 1975. She claims that her marketing technique is the key to her success. She buys her stock at a discount — after retail stores have stopped buying from the manufacturers, but not before consumers have stopped adding to their wardrobe. Selling 10 to 50 per cent below manufacturers' retail prices, she bought from 100 manufacturers in 1986. Her independent sales coordinators running home parties put up a deposit of $500 in exchange for about $7,000 worth of inventory, including garment bags and display racks. A sales coordinator working, typically, two to three evenings a week, may earn from $10,000 to $40,000 a year. Nichol pays a percentage of the sales volume produced by the coordinator, plus a bonus after reaching a sales target. It is easy to spot the ways in which the company has taken advantage of change — in seasons and in fashion, in numbers of working women, and in the need for additional family income.

It may have been the recession that gave her the biggest help. While retailers were laying off staff, buyers turned to the one-to-one attention found in home fashion parties. We all like to be served, and resent having to wait or stand in line with our cold hard cash, before someone even asks if they can help. This service orientation has propelled Pirjo-Liisa Fashions Ltd. from a home fashion party service to a fifteen-store retail outlet.

Nichol's success is based on market assessment — knowing who will buy what you have to sell. Unless you can pinpoint who will buy at what price, when and why, you may not have a business. Like any other part of your business, the marketing of your goods or services must be planned. This chapter is devoted to the planning stage.

Your Marketing Strategy: A Questionnaire

The development of a marketing strategy is a key step in the establishment of an enterprise. The following questionnaire from *Entrepreneurship: A Primer for Canadians* summarizes the main factors an entrepreneur should consider when undertaking a market analysis.

Your Customers:

What are they? Age, sex, income bracket.
Where do they live, play, shop?
What motivates them to buy your products?
How often do they buy? Seasonally?
Do they use cash or credit?
Can you afford to carry accounts receivable?

Your Competition:

How big, how old, how strong are they?
What percentage of the market do they have?
How far away are they?
What advantages do they have?
What disadvantages do they have?
What percentage of the market will you get?

Your Products:

Are they unique, eye-appealing?
Are they better designed, higher quality?
What sizes and special packaging do they have?
Is there a need for your products?
Must you offer a guarantee?
What will be your returns policy?
Must you stock parts for service?

Pricing:

Do you know what to charge to cover your costs?
Are your prices competitive?
How important is low price?
Is service more important?
Must you give discounts for cash, volume, distributors, salespeople?
What will discounts do to your mark up?
Must you include delivery cost in your price?

Advertising:

How much is normal for your products?
Which media should you use? How often? Seasonally?
Do you have a logo or trademark? Is it registered?

Is any free publicity available?
Will you need an advertising agency?

Buying:
How much of each will you buy? From whom?
Are you getting the best deal?
Is volume discount eaten up by slow turnover?
Can you return unsold merchandise?
Have you a stock-control plan to avoid overstocks, understocks, and out-of-stocks?
Have you established a line of credit with each supplier?
How must you pay — COD, thirty days, sixty days?

Distribution:
If you are a manufacturer, how will you sell — through dealers, distributors, sales agents, or direct to the consumer?
What is common in the industry?
Do transportation costs dictate the best method of distribution?

Successful marketing then is the result of five major elements:

1. an understanding of the need for your product or service;
2. a well-researched and properly evaluated marketplace;
3. matching your product or service to meet the pre-determined market niche;
4. efficient production of product or service;
5. effective communication to the market segment.

Identifying Your Customers
A company's most effective use of marketing can only result from identifying your potential customers. Companies with large research budgets make use of research houses which usually charge thousands of dollars. You may be able to find someone at a local community college or university who would be willing to take on the research for credit. A friend of mine recently started a radio station in a major Canadian market and did just that to monitor her listening audience.

Data is also available from the following sources:

1. Yellow Pages
2. Statistics Canada
3. City or Municipal Hall
4. Telephone surveys
5. On-the-spot surveys
6. Newspapers and magazines
7. Trade publications
8. Competition
9. Trade associations
10. Chambers of Commerce and Boards of Trade
11. Shopping centre developers
12. Radio and television
13. Downtown business associations and women's associations
14. Colleges and universities
15. Libraries
16. Regional, provincial, or federal government offices

Pinpointing the Variables

A marketing plan should take into account variables — changes that you know will be happening as well as those you may not have had an opportunity to plan for in advance. Changes can take place in any market that will affect the volume of business either in a negative or positive way. What you must realize is that there will always be changes both internal (within your company) and external, which you may or may not have any control over.

Some of the external changes over which you may have control for planning purposes might be: seasons, holidays, special events, fashions, or styles. To adjust to other external factors, you may need substantially more lead time; for example, shifts in population densities, political events, government budgets, weather, gross national product, consumer earnings, rate of inflation, and unemployment.

Internal changes may well be in the form of product changes (in style or quality, or in volume of production), price changes, packaging and promotional shifts, and inventory shortages or surplus.

Promotion Plans

Keep in mind that the big picture is called marketing. Promotion is getting the message out. Preparing a promotion calendar a year ahead will tell you where you are going. Let's take, for example, a small retail operation specializing in uniforms for the health-care industry. You may want to prepare a promotion budget like this: January — semi-annual clearance; February — after-white sale on uniforms only; March — get ready for spring by promoting uniforms in the newest spring colours, and so on.

Another example is Vancouver-based Cookies by George. By volume they are the biggest producer of cookies in Canada. When the company was started by Tera and Gayle Hallgren along with friend Noreen Kenny-Campbell three years ago, they had a great concept but, seemingly, not a heck of a lot else working on their side. In the first place, they were going against an already firmly entrenched health-food trend. In 1981 people were talking calories and nutrition, not cookies. But because of clever marketing, advertising, and promotion, they not only own six corporate stores, but also have six franchise operations as well. While their product may be cookies, what they are in fact producing is a gourmet treat. And that is the way they are marketed all over the world. The importance of their marketing strategy was commented on by one acute businessman who remarked, when observing them in a prestigious shopping mall, "Your cookies must be very special. They occupy their own piece of real estate." They have made the lowly cookie glamorous by marketing it as a distinguished specialty item with its own unique outlet.

Advertising

The advertising budget is integral to your promotion plans. For different ventures it will vary as much as the ventures themselves. Generally, in a small retail operation a figure of 2.5 per cent of the total sales could be spent on advertising, a medium retailer could consider about 3.5 per cent, and the very large operation about 2.5 per cent. The newer the store, the more advertising will be required to bring it to the public's attention. The location for any store is critical. A bad location can generate a need for more advertising dollars. Because of the competition, it is safe to assume that a merchant in a large metropolis would have to spend more dollars to grab the needed market share. A very large, well-established firm does not need to make its presence felt as much as a small one does.

Frequency of advertising is always a big question. The guideline is: advertising expenditures should be emphasized just before the time when business will be greatest. The months of October and November are critical to some firms for Christmas profits. Some businesses' sales bottom out in January and February, so don't bother wasting your advertising dollars then — people probably can't be convinced to spend. Lack of money on the part of the consumer is always a concern of business during recessionary times. You should be sure you can make your advertising money back in the form of increased sales *before* you spend it.

Your advertising plan for any time period should answer six basic questions, as in the following example.

Easter Advertising Plan
Promotional Calendar for March 15-30 Campaign

QUESTION	ACTION
What?	Cookies
When?	1. Easter — Happy Easter Basket 2. request of corporate clients (e.g., Apple Computers — packaging of apples and cookies) 3. Thank Goodness It's George Days (when Cookies by George allows schools to purchase its cookies at a discount for students to resell in support of a particular activity)
Why?	to be visible to be part of the community to create basis for increased sales
Who?	Yuppies, teenagers; create an adult cookie market

Where? radio campaigns (sponsor weather report),local papers, promotions with product itself

How? utilize 3 per cent of gross sales, actually 10 per cent including lost revenue and cost of promotion

Keep in mind that this represents basic information only. Your plan must incorporate dates, as well as amounts budgeted for each item.

The APIC Approach

As a new entrepreneur you may not have the budget of a large, well-established business. Working well within your budget will be the result of preparing and executing your marketing plan properly. The following represents a guideline you'll find helpful. An easy way to remember this step-by-step theory is to remember the acronym APIC.

A — Analysis

Analyze your business. What are the tangible results of my product or service? Why would someone want to make use of what I have to offer? What are my major strengths and weaknesses?

P — Planning

Planning your marketing strategy is necessary and is expressed in terms of time and money. Make the objectives realistic ones that will assure you a sense of accomplishment. Keep in mind that planning is based on research, not guesswork. Find ways to blow the competition out of the water.

I — Implementation

By this stage you really are in business. You now put your plan into action by offering your product or service to those you've identified as ready, willing, and able to buy. It's conceivable selling cookies would go like this:

Ready Chocolate chip cookie lovers and those willing to be converted.

Willing Those desirous of a superior cookie and attracted to creative packaging to justify the price.

Able Those with money who have the luxury of buying quality (if not always quantity).

C — Control

Control calls for good, solid attention to detail. What Tera and Gayle and Noreen are able to do is execute control beyond the product and the packaging. What is interesting in this trio is that they are equally conversant with all aspects of the business and can change roles — finance, creative, production, marketing, management — depending on corporate needs. Their corporation is computerized, giving them immediate access to current information and better control over both corporate and franchise businesses. How they baked $2 million worth of cookies in about three years makes a study for any marketing textbook. What strikes you immediately is their great packaging. They rely on basic bakery boxes, expensive ribbon, and a card dedicated to the occasion. They reach the market like this:

1. They put eighteen cookies in a florist's box with a huge bow and a card reading "Because you can't eat flowers." Cost: $12.00.
2. For that special someone in your life who's being a real crumb, a box of cookie crumbs is delivered anonymously with a card reading "You crumb." Cost: $6.00.
3. Then, of course, there's always the other person of note in your life. A box of twelve cookies is tagged "May this romance last longer than these cookies." Cost: $7.50.

They know their market is at two ends of the scale: those with excessive income, who think nothing of paying a premium price for a good cookie, and those with a limited one who choose to splurge occasionally for what they feel is quality versus quantity. Typing, or separating, customers is called market segmentation. This is very important for the new or relatively new entrepreneur, because it will be impossible to please everyone.

Once you've decided on your marketing plan, it is time to put it to work. The next chapter constitutes a crash course in implementation.

Chapter 6

CREATING A DEMAND FOR YOUR PRODUCT

We have not had to go out there and beat the bushes. People were approaching us long before we franchised.

Mellanie Stephens, President, Kettle Creek Canvas Co.

While you may think that Mellanie Stephens (quoted on the previous page) is in an enviable position, it is one you can create yourself. Word-of-mouth is the best form of advertising. But if your company is relatively new, there may not yet be the opportunity for that. Or worse still, what if your product is your service and there are fifty people in your city providing exactly the same? Your challenge is to let them know you are out there and that you provide the best. You can do this through successful implementation of your marketing plan.

While it may not be polite to run down your competition, you are going to have to adopt a Muhammad Ali philosophy. People in business who are not convinced that they are the best will never succeed. You've probably heard of the entrepreneur who identified a need and set up a business (complete with cards, telephone, office, stationery, and lots of order forms), only to discover that the world did not beat a path to her door. The world wasn't even aware of the door! While you may not have to pull your customers off the sidewalk, you do have to do something.

Advertising

While some businesses never spend a marketing dollar without the blessing of an advertising, promotion, or public-relations guru, many small businesses simply cannot afford to hire one. If you find yourself in this position, you'll want to arm yourself with the best information possible to make the best use of your advertising and promotion dollars.

Marketing combines sales, advertising, public relations, sales promotion, packaging, and direct mail — anything connected with the sale of the product or service. It is advertising that deals with creating the need or desire to buy the product or service by using a variety of media (time, space, bus benches, and so forth). To use them you'll need the North American media-buyer's bibles — *Canadian Advertising Rates and Data* (about $75 per issue), updated monthly by Maclean Hunter, and *Standard Rates and Data*, which is published in the United States. These directories contain the names, circulations, and advertising costs of all newspapers and magazines, both business and trade, in North America, as well as TV and radio stations. Publications are listed by category and simplify media selection. You may want to look into another Maclean Hunter publication called *Survey of Markets*, a dandy guide offering significant demographic information for each marketing area in every province of Canada.

Whether you are personally in charge of your advertising, or choose to make use of an agency, here are some guidelines. Do not make advertising a hit-and-miss decision. *Make an advertising plan.* It is a component of your marketing plan, and without it you are in trouble. It is a guide to advertising expenditures and serves as a form of control over those expenditures. It should work for you in the following ways: it should relate your advertising to your overall marketing objectives and it should spell out those budgets, keeping control over careless spending by allowing for pre-testing of new products and services. It will provide for the repetition of successful promotions; allow you to focus on trends, events, and seasons; and allow you to work in conjunction with, or around, your competitors' activities.

This year's advertising plan is based on a combination of last year's experience and your best judgement of the upcoming year's prospects. In the case of a new business, it is none of the former and all of the latter. The Advertising Plan is designed to do four things for your business: build public awareness; legitimize the business; break down by dollars, season, and month where your advertising and promotional dollars are going; and provide a methodical direction for you and your business, while assuring the public that you are still in business. It is important to remember that all businesses allocate a percentage of their budget to helping them grow through advertising.

The Seven Ds

Let's take a look at what I call Examining Your Ds Before You Invest.

1. Decide the overall objective.
   Is this advertisement part of a long-range marketing plan? Is it part of a marketing or sales objective or a last-minute whim?

2. Distinguish the specific objective.
   What do you intend this advertising to accomplish? Sell more computers, cookies, lingerie, Christmas tree lights? Is it to announce a new product or service? Every ad should have a primary purpose.
3. Dig up the facts.
   Know your product or service. Know the benefits, rewards, costs, ingredients, capabilities, life, or service.
4. Detect the appeal.
   What is unique or different, better or newer, cleaner or longer-lasting about your product or service? Why have customers and clients made use of it in the past? Why you and not the competition?
5. Designate the medium.
   How can your story best be told? How about someone reading the newspaper, driving past a billboard, watching a late-night movie, listening to the radio, finding a flyer in the mail?
6. Design the message to suit the medium.
   Each medium imposes its own set of restrictions. In radio, it's time; in print, it's space; on television, it's time and visuals restricted by budget.
7. Determine the viability before you spend your money. Seek the help of someone who has the experience (buy, beg, or barter) before you commit to spending. If all else fails, follow your instincts.

Running Your Own Campaign

In the event that you have decided to tackle this whole business of advertising and promotion yourself, you'll be pleased to know that most magazine, business publications, and radio and television stations make available to their customers some form of media kit. In the case of radio and TV, it may only be a rate card, but publications frequently offer a full media kit, containing the card showing advertising rates (both national and local), frequency discounts (either for saturation or long-term advertising), copy and material preparation requirements, and a demographic study of their circulation.

Let's take a look at the three most common media used to get those dollars rolling in. First there's print, and it applies to flyers, magazine ads, and brochures and will need a real grabber to be effective. You simply have to get the reader's attention. Keep the English simple (some sources say Grade 6 level); it must be clear and concise. Display advertising is show-and-tell in print. You will pay a premium to make use of display placement (ads that are not in the classified section of the newspaper or magazine), but you may be able to justify the additional cost. What display advertising does is allow the "specific" placement of your message in the section most likely to attract the customers you want — for example, food, fashion, business. When thinking in terms of print media, for most small retail or service businesses (even some very small manufacturing businesses), community newspapers work very well, and they are generally free to the consuming public. While ads in the classified section cost less money, they don't command as much attention. Nevertheless, they are an inexpensive way to reach your market. These ads have a fixed price for a specified number of lines, with a charge per word thereafter. Consider them a good way to test the market, or to saturate your message week after week at a minimal cost.

If you are just beginning to advertise and are doing the buying or placing the ads yourself, take advantage of the free advice given by people in the advertising departments of newspapers and magazines. Do some sleuthing for yourself and examine current ads to determine what makes them jump off the pages. Take a look at publications to determine their reach, or how many people subscribe over a given period of time, as well as the market they are hitting. Is it yours?

Remember the old David Ogilvy (a giant in American advertising) "KISS principle" as it applies to advertising — Keep It Simple, Stupid. By that he meant, forget sophisticated language, puns, and subtle nuances. Don't dance around the message. Spell it out, simply, clearly, concisely. Edit, trim, and keep it straightforward. Brilliance does not sell — facts do. Focus on the dominant feature and help the consumer make a decision. If you are using graphics, photographs generally work best; inaccurate renderings may lead to problems with a little matter called truth in advertising.

Misleading, false, unfair, or exaggerated advertising claims (however portrayed) come under the protection of the federal Department of Consumer and Corporate Affairs. Besides that, various advertising media have each established codes of ethics to screen out messages that are misleading or in bad taste. Keep in mind that when you're promoting your business, you're selling yourself as well.

Radio is a fun and medium-priced way to get the message across in either thirty or sixty seconds. Radio stations are always having promotions and package deals. It may be that you have a product or service the radio station can use as free prizes. You might want to contact the sales manager and offer your product in exchange for air mentions during a station promotion. Whenever possible, take advantage of the times when rates are generally cheaper. If you or someone you know has good copywriting skills, you can provide the copy yourself; otherwise, let the station or your ad agency do it for you. An unprofessional ad on the air will sound amateurish and will do your business more harm than good. We've all heard bad copy and genuinely felt sorry for the person paying for the ad.

What is even worse, in my judgement, is the person who insists on voicing her own commercial. Unless your voice is radio-quality, or so unique that people would positively associate it with your business, leave the ad's voice to the professionals at the station, or have it booked through your agency. What happens in this case is that an agency will hire a professional to voice your commercial, leaving you with the option of buying out the voice used (a one-time payment). Alternatively, the agency will call for residuals every time the commercial is aired. This happens in both radio and television.

Several years ago I did a commercial for Shoppers Drug Mart; quarterly, like clockwork, my cheques arrived for a full three years after the shoot. For you, the advertiser, we're looking at big bucks. If you have the budget, make use of an agency to guide you as well as recommend your advertising budget. An advertising agency is in a position to sell you artwork for ads and brochures and will generally charge by the hour. They are also in a position to book media. If using an agency is out of the question, budget-wise, take it upon yourself to make advertising one more area of continuous growth for you and your company. Start reading publications like *Advertising Age*, an American weekly, and Maclean Hunter's weekly publication *Marketing* magazine. While you may not have the advertising budget of some of the corporate giants featured on their glossy pages, remember that the concept for Cookies by George originated in New York, long before it was brought to Vancouver. These publications may provide the creative spark for your next business or next ad.

Television ads, also sold in slots of sixty seconds and thirty seconds, are the most expensive, but if handled well they can be the most effective. In keeping with the idea that nothing is new under the sun, we're beginning to see a trickle of black-and-white ads. They are cheaper to produce, stir up nostalgia, and get your attention simply because, in the eighties, black-and-white is different.

In TV ads, stick to one main idea. Keep the language simple and the sentences short. Don't philosophize. Make it believable. Allow the visuals and the words to tell the story. Don't try to be *Saturday Night Live* or (for those who remember) *Laugh In*. Few people have the talent and skills to pull off comedy. Comedy badly done is downright annoying. Again, if you are not going through an advertising agency, trust the people at the TV station. Be very clear about the message you need to get across. Make sure you have final approval for script and visuals, but understand that the people at the station or agency have probably done thousands of commercials, so give them a chance. They probably know what will and will not be effective better than you do.

Having worked in all three media, I've witnessed costly mistakes made because of lack of attention to detail, lack of clarity in the message, and the client's inflated ego which overrode sound professional advice. All such mistakes result in needless waste of advertising dollars. Know that your business is what you are good at — leave radio, television, and print whenever possible to the specialists. Most production and layout is included in the fees anyway. Don't be a jerk!

A word of caution about all three forms. If an ad is printed on the wrong day, or a commercial run at the wrong time (or maybe it gets garbled), you have the right to demand what is called a "make good." In other words, they have to make good their error to you, usually by running the ad again.

You may want to advertise in the Yellow Pages. There are two good reasons to do so. First, there in black and yellow is an instant potential client base. Second, it is a highly visible place for your business to be discovered by virtually every householder, and certainly every business, in your town or across the country. But be careful about your financial commitment. Most businesses require only a line or two. Unless you are absolutely certain of the classification you belong under, discuss it with the phone company's representative just to make sure. For example, if you are a business consultant and that is all you do, the solution is simple. Advertise under the section headed *Business Consultants.* But what about the woman whose career objective is to be Canada's hottest fashion designer? If her actual cashflow comes from doing alterations and colour analysis, with a limited budget, where does she spend those Yellow Page dollars? In a situation like this, I'd vote for advertising under *Colour Analysis* rather than *Alterations*. Here's why. The cost per analysis, per hour, has a current going rate of about $50 to $75. The price of turning a hem is about $15 for approximately the same amount of work. Why not advertise under *Colour Analysis*, or as close as your Yellow Page listings will allow, and add to the ad "alterations" and "one-of-a-kind-fashion design"?

You may want to further investigate the cost of multiple listings, and maybe look at the cost of a good display ad. A caution here. Make sure you are in a position to pay that advertising expense throughout the year. It will be billed to you along with your regular business phone expenses month after month. You will not have the opportunity to say "I can't afford it" in October, when the new book comes out in June. It's a decision you'll have to make for yourself. The Yellow Pages are beyond the advertising reach of many consultants, who consider word-of-mouth their most important marketing vehicle.

In the event that you have a retail operation, one of the best forms of advertising is a great window display. Customer interviews indicate that most purchasers window-shop before entering a store. While it may be easy to blame poor location or lack of drop-in trade for poor sales, it is a fact that great windows will draw customers. Everyone is attracted to beauty. If you don't believe me, consider your childhood drives to the classier sections of town at Christmas time, to see the beautiful, Christmas-tree-lit windows.

Planning your window display requires no less precision than the rest of your advertising. Change displays often. Do not show price tags except perhaps in the case of an exceptional mark down or feature, and keep to one central theme. Hire your little brother to count the numbers of passers-by who glance, look, or seem drawn to and eventually land in your store. In larger cities there are people available who, for a price, will decorate your windows for you. You may want to investigate a local community college or high school with courses in window dressing either for you, or your staff, or hire a student.

Public Relations

Public relations agencies offer many vehicles for "free" advertising — for a price. A news release can be an effective and inexpensive vehicle for getting people's attention. The key to its success is in making it interesting. Do this by determining why in the world someone would want to read it, talk to you about it, write about what you have to offer, or invite you to join them on a talk show. Media people know that there is very little new under the sun. The press release must grab their attention before they'll consider the item newsworthy. You will need to spell out who you are, what you have to offer, and why they should pay attention to you. Perhaps you are having a grand opening, or have a revolutionary product in the marketplace, a solution to an old problem, or anything else you feel will make them want to get involved. Don't forget to give them a contact name and telephone number for additional information. Available are a number of good how-to books on the writing of releases, or you may want to have yours written professionally.

Once the release is in the mail, follow it up a few days later with a phone call to make sure it got into the hands of someone who is in a position to do something about it. Don't be self-conscious about bugging people. They may be interested, but may not have had an opportunity to get back to you, or may be uninterested and this is your opportunity to sell them on what you have to offer. Of course, you will have called ahead to make sure of the proper person to mail it to, along with the correct spelling of the name and title.

Keep in mind that we all love to be flattered. When sending your release to media personalities, tell them how much you appreciate them, their work, and the time they are taking to consider your release.

I call this next piece of advice, Advice for the Terrified. The whole purpose of the news release is to get your company some press — radio, television, print — free. The first word of advice on your eventual interview is to say absolutely nothing you would not like to hear on the radio, read in print, or hear and see on television. Once you find someone to interview you, make sure you know not only the inside and outside of your business, but also exactly what you are prepared to say, regardless of how they phrase the questions. It's a good idea to present beforehand (even pop it in the mail) questions you like to be asked. Should you be asked questions you don't want to answer, rephrase that question so it suits what you want to say. Keep in mind one single, important fact that will promote your business well and make sure that, whether they ask for it or not, you say it at least twice. It's always a good idea to preface your statement with something like, "What is unique about what I am doing is," or, if you have an accounting business, "What taxpayers should know about taxes is." It is imperative that you take control of the message you want to get out, or all the paper and postage and anxiety over the interview will have been for nothing.

A public relations agency, if you can afford one, will write your release and post it, follow it up with phone calls, and arrange media bookings. A good agency — and you should shop around and talk to clients — will know the best places to send your particular release and the best places for your business to be promoted.

Public Speaking

In case you'd rather be sick, you may want to refer to author Jack Valenti's *Speak Up — Speak Out*. In it he refers to public speaking being Public Fear #1 — apparently right up there with death and taxes. A number of years ago I ran a class called "Speaking for Scaredy-cats," and believe me, they showed up in droves. You are probably telling yourself right now, "But I can't."

For eight years as a child I talked in front of mirrors because I stammered so badly that no one could understand me. Of course, like most people overcoming a handicap, once I got started . . . well, I still can't stop. At age thirteen, I won my first public speaking contest. Years ago, when I got my first radio program, my mother's remarks said it all: "At least now I get to turn you off." It was a very bumpy ride for me, learning to speak, but eventually the process of putting one word after another became easier and easier. It takes desire, determination, and lots of practice.

Back to the scaredy-cats. Here are a few guidelines:

1. Know your subject thoroughly.
2. Be convinced that absolutely everyone in your audience is going to love you.
3. If you can't cope with eye-to-eye contact with real people, imagine your audience is comprised of heads of cabbage. If that doesn't help, pretend everyone in your audience is nude —that way, they'll be feeling more self-conscious than you are.
4. Wear your most comfortable clothing (that includes shoes).
5. If you are going to speak after a meal — don't eat, just nibble. Food requires energy to be digested. And please, don't have an alcoholic drink. You only think you'll be relaxed!
6. Take a few deep breaths, preferably in through your mouth and out through your nose.
7. Before you open your mouth, allow yourself to collect your thoughts and your energy. Face your audience. Find a kind (or sexy) pair of eyes, and begin.
8. Start out by speaking slowly and saying all your *T*s and *D*s and *-ings* at the ends of your words. That in itself will slow you down. Most nervous people tend to speak far too quickly.
9. Should you start blowing it or making a series of noticeable mistakes, stop, pause, regain your control, and begin again.
10. Try to have a good time and sell yourself, product, or service.

Now that you've got the fear under control and the confidence in hand, there are a number of ways to use speaking as a way of promoting yourself. Seminars, workshops, and other ways to get people to listen are excellent promotional tools. Handle them right and they can be income-producing as well. Even if you decide to charge, remember that Art Linkletter still does freebies.

The concept of carroting works like a gem. Give a free workshop or seminar, serve an inexpensive refreshment, and sell, sell, sell them on an all-day event. A good time frame is a Friday evening in promotion of a weekend event (same weekend) or a lecture on a Monday, with paid follow-up on Thursday. Don't let too much time pass. Get them while they're hot and be aware that most people get paid either in the middle or at the end of the month. Have your promotional material on hand so they can express immediate, qualified interest and part with their money at the same time.

Depending on your business, most non-profit organizations are always looking for luncheon speakers. This is generally the rubber-chicken circuit, and although you don't get paid, they feed you and provide a captive audience. Just make sure you have plenty of business cards on hand, smile a lot, and leave plenty of time for questions and answers so you can impress on them how professional you are. Please, please, make a point of telling your audience that what you are doing is your business and that you welcome their business. There's nothing pushy about it. Besides, you have so much to offer.

I hate to say it but, because you are a woman, you may have more than your share of opportunities to promote your business through public appearances. The issue of women in business has made a whole lot of men nervous, and others merely hope to see us fall on our faces. By simply telling them about your product or service, and backing it up with a few facts, you will have informed them and you'll look wonderfully bright, like the independent, self-reliant person that you are. Be careful not to get in over your head. Don't say anything you can't back up, but throwing in a few well-placed, brilliant lines never hurts. Do know your competition in the marketplace, but never, under any circumstances, criticize them in public. Phrases such as "It is my understanding,'' ''According to my research,'' and ''Perhaps'' make statements on their own. Remember that there is power in silence.

Other Alternatives

The number of ways to promote your business is limited only by your imagination. Here are some of the more common ways beyond those we have already reviewed:

flyers — mailed or hand-distributed
loudspeaker announcements
demos
sales presentations
endorsements
corporate ID programs
premiums
product publicity
free samples
point-of-sale displays
film
packaging
sales conferences
trade exhibits
catalogues

It is not uncommon for entrepreneurs with small consulting practices (or those who teach a specific skill) to teach night school as well. Most cities have community colleges, universities, and certainly a YWCA. Then, of course, you may try to arrange something with your church or synagogue — you may not get paid for your work, but it will help you to get your name, service, and reputation out there to those who can and will pay.

It is important for you to do some form of promotion to tell the community you're out there. You may want to invite a number of people over to your office or business for some wine and cheese. A little wine, a little cheese, and a few crispy crackers can say anything from ''I appreciate your business,'' to ''Welcome to my new location,'' or, ''Why in the heck aren't you making more use of me?'' It does not have to be lavish, but it should take place.

To me, advertising is like one big musical production. What gets to me is all the glitter, costuming, music, and staging. A business without promotion and advertising is like a musical without the tap dancing. No action, no energy. Razzmatazz never goes out of style.

Some other ways to promote yourself are:

1. *Networking*. It provides good emotional and business support, especially for people new to the entrepreneurial role. Remember, it can take a whole lot of cups of coffee to cement a business transaction.
2. *Professional affiliations*. Through them you learn the latest product update and resources for funding. You know what your competition is doing and find new business contacts.
3. *Chamber of Commerce lists*. These will vary in availability and form depending on the community.
4. *Newspaper items*. The business and financial pages often carry items on the arrival of new business or industries. They also tell of appointments of executives who may be in a position to buy multiple enrollments or company classes. Some libraries maintain a file of news clippings on local companies. Read papers and magazines relating to your particular industry.
5. *Professional mailing lists*. These are available through national, provincial, county, or local associations. Get on them and make use of them to reach your customers. Private customers also offer mailing lists.
6. *Rosters of organizations*. The Chamber of Commerce frequently has these rosters. Chamber members belong to all kinds of organizations. Be alert while talking to them and ask for rosters of groups that they belong to; you will find they are usually glad to give you the rosters.
7. *Neighbourhood hikes*. Go down the street and stop in at attractive stores and offices. This is by far the toughest, but sometimes the most rewarding, type of prospecting. It takes time and courage and lots of bother, but it works. A variation of this method is to go through the yellow pages of the telephone book and call for appointments.

8. *Trade publications*. These are available in office lobbies, libraries, and by subscription. They are easily obtained and produce worthwhile prospects. Companies that advertise in them are the more progressive ones.
9. *Information exchange group*. A number of such groups exist — better still, start your own.
10. *Community newspapers*. These are great for free publicity. Ads are lower-priced than those in major market papers, and regular advertisers usually get preferential treatment in feature articles.

Chapter 7

WHAT YOU NEED IS A TEAM

I finally hired an accountant after about six months in business.

Ardith Scrutton,
A.J. Copyrite Printing and Typesetting

Put off hiring an accountant in some businesses, and you're out of business. You will be called on to play numerous roles during your start-up years, so leave the professional part of your business to the professionals. I am thinking specifically of three: your banker, your lawyer, and your accountant. Think of them as key players on your winning team. Because a team is exactly what you will need. Behind every self-made, successful entrepreneur are a number of players who helped make the winning possible. It may be useful for you to think of your business-team players as similar to those in a game of football.

Components of the Entrepreneurial Team

The game	A profit-producing business.
The rules	Make use of your own experience, talent, and skills. Hire the best talent you can afford. Play to win.
Coach	You, the entrepreneur.
Starting line-up	Banker, lawyer, accountant.
Cheerleaders	Family and close friends.
Cheering section	Business associations, clubs, organizations, strong network of associates.
Ballfield	Business location.
Equipment	Product or service.
Fans	Your market.
Tickets/passes	Marketing techniques.
Time out	Course redirection, redefinition of goals, possible expansion or cutback.
Referee	Business advisor.

Because your team will be essential for your success, you will want to choose it wisely. Deciding who would make a good player, and when to let them be part of the action, is something you will have to do for yourself. Here are guidelines in the selection of your three key players: your lawyer, your banker, your accountant.

Your Lawyer

Be sure to choose a lawyer whose specialty is business law

(preferably small business). I know of one woman who made use of her divorce lawyer! Do yourself a favour and go lawyer shopping (yes, shopping) before you start your business. Many women try to cut corners, particularly at the outset of the business, by by-passing the services of a lawyer. Don't. Your lawyer should be well versed in contract law and you should avoid after-the-fact advice. For example, don't call a lawyer to ask advice after you have signed a five-year rental agreement. Depending on your type of business, you may be in need of a variety of standard contracts to be used with your clients and suppliers. The initial legal cost is probably worth a good night's sleep in the future. Be specific when asking about fees for services. You will need to know about hourly rates as well as costs for specific work such as filing fees, ordering documents, or the drawing up of contracts.

Choose a lawyer with whom you feel at ease. He or she will be on your team for a long time. The freedom to pick up the phone and ask on-the-spot advice is important. Remember that with all their unfamiliar jargon, lawyers are in the marketplace to earn a living just like you. Ask for recommendations from friends who own small businesses of lawyers they feel are caring and supportive of small business. Keep in mind that the job of a lawyer is to give you objective, professional advice, and anything less will not do.

When deciding what type of legal entity your business should be, use the advice of a lawyer as well as an accountant. The following is a simple chart listing the advantages and disadvantages of the three forms of business most often used. It is adapted from William Jennings's publication, *Entrepreneurship: A Primer for Canadians*.

Forms of Business Classification

ADVANTAGES	*DISADVANTAGES*
Sole Proprietorship Also known as self-employment.	
1. Low start-up costs	1. Unlimited liability

2. Greatest freedom from regulations
3. Owner in direct control
4. Minimal working capital requirements
5. Tax advantage to small owner
6. All profits to owner

2. Lack of continuity
3. Difficult to raise capital

Partnership

Can be silent or active, depending on partnership agreement.

1. Ease of formation
2. Low start-up costs
3. Additional sources of venture capital
4. Broader management base
5. Possible tax advantage
6. Limited outside regulation

1. Unlimited liability
2. Lack of continuity
3. Divided authority
4. Difficulty in raising additional capital
5. Hard to find suitable partners

Corporation

Or Limited Company. You may be the sole employee of your corporation.

1. Limited liability
2. Specialized management
3. Ownership is transferable
4. Continuous existence
5. Legal entity
6. Possible tax advantage
7. Easier to raise capital

1. Closely regulated
2. Most expensive form to organize
3. Charter restrictions
4. Extensive record keeping
5. Double taxation

Note: Advantages and disadvantages may vary from province to province. Be certain to get professional advice.

Your Accountant

Time was when small-business owners could make use of bookkeeping services only. But today, the financial needs of business are not only so complex, but are also changing so rapidly, that you need the most sophisticated advice you can afford. Most small businesses make use of both a bookkeeper and an accountant — usually a chartered accountant (CA). A chartered accountant will set up your company books and provide tax assistance, auditing, general accounting, and financial statements. A CA is also in a position to help you with financial, investment, and tax planning.

Whether you choose the services of an independent practitioner specializing in small business or use the services of a major accounting firm with a portion of its services devoted to small business, shop before you decide. Once again, ask friends and associates who they make use of. Just remember that the accountant should have knowledge of your type of business. The least expensive accountant may in fact deliver the poorest performance. Some entrepreneurs make use of certified general accountants (CGAs) instead, for additional management or financial consulting. Be sure always to ask for a fee structure, and expect a letter of engagement spelling out exactly what they are prepared to do for your investment. One woman, when talking about her need for an accountant, put it this way: "I started my business on a part-time basis and operated from my home, therefore overhead was not high. As the business grew so did my cashflow, enabling me to expand. I think it's important not to go into heavy debt or overhead costs in the beginning, nor to depend on large bank loans because of overextended finances. Too many women in my industry [fashion] think running a store is just playing with clothes. The best retailers today are good accountants. Know your strengths and weaknesses in business by hiring people for areas in which you may not excel. Learn to separate the emotional from the business aspect of your life."

It is important not to live under the false impression that a good accountant will lessen your chances of being audited. If you are audited, fulfilling your legal obligations by keeping good books will be more important than ever. As a business owner, you (not your accountant) are responsible for keeping track of every source of income and expense your venture incurs. At any time, you should be able to look at your books and know exactly where your company stands financially. Understanding the bottom line on that financial statement will give you an enhanced feeling of control as well as commitment to your company.

Your Banker

How much easier it would be if every woman launching a business could make the statement of one successful entrepreneur: "We were fortunate to have strong management ability and knew how to prepare a presentation for the bank." Whether you approach a lending institution first or last in your team-building effort, you should understand that there are two types of financing, equity and borrowed money. In Chapter 2 we talked about equity; it is all the money you have now, from sources such as savings, assets, property, and investments if any. You may need to supplement your equity with money from a lending institution.

Your banker is in such a key position that, without his or her support and cooperation, the chances of your business succeeding may be minimal. Good communication is essential. There is an old saying: the only time a bank will lend you money is when you don't need it. Not necessarily so today. Financial institutions such as insurance conglomerates and accounting houses are well aware that women are among Canada's best and brightest entrepreneurs. They are aware, too, that women's business survival rate surpasses that of their male counterparts. Translation? They are willing to share in your profits.

Shop for a banker who knows and understands the challenge of small business. Find yourself a lender who understands your type of venture. Shop for lending institutions as you would for a pair of shoes. Go ahead — *put that foot in*. I know of one woman who, before putting her foot in the door, finds out the location of the manager's office and observes it for a few minutes a couple of days before the interview, just to get a sense of whom she will be dealing with. Do not let a lending institution choose you. You do the choosing. Talk with managers and lending officers. Compare rates, policies, locations, accessibility of the manager, hours of operation, lines of credit, spousal guarantees (that's when they ask for your husband's signature on the dotted line), and ability to service small businesses adequately.

In all fairness to lending institutions, spousal guarantees are controversial. When Diana Ferguson started Berwick Ferguson Payroll Canada Ltd. in 1975, a company with annual sales now approaching $1 million, she put together a plan, went to the bank, told the manager how much money she wanted, why she wanted it, what she expected to get out of it, and supplied anticipated results in terms of market research. She got her loan — with her husband's signature. But as she told Catherine Kentridge of *Small Business*, ''Any time you borrow money, the bank would rather have a co-signer or guarantor, no matter who you are. It doesn't care whether the co-signer's a husband, father, wife, sister, or pygmy. It just wants someone who's good for the guarantee . . . . When I started, I didn't have any assets except my brains, but the bank wasn't about to do a deal based on them.'' Today, Ferguson is in the position to sign on the dotted line for others. About 495 of the *Financial Post* 500 are on her client list. Of course, the flip side of the coin is when a woman does have the ability to repay and is still subjected to this requirement. It happens.

At the time of the interview (assuming you have done your financial homework — business plan, marketing plan, cashflow projections) keep mental notes on the following:

1. Do I feel comfortable or do I feel intimidated?
2. Does this person understand my type of business?
3. Is this person approachable?
4. Do I feel a sense of trust and respect for and from this person?
5. Would I feel more comfortable dealing with someone of the same or the opposite sex?
6. Am I convinced I have chosen the right lender?
7. If refused, am I being told why (lack of experience, age, education, collateral or equity; inadequate presentation)?

Make sure you have a friend, an associate, or your accountant go over your presentation to the bank *with you* beforehand. The amount of serious attention you receive will be directly proportionate to the amount of preparation you put into the business plan. You may want to bring your accountant along if you are unfamiliar with banking jargon and financial statements; otherwise, you may feel confident enough to go alone. Canadians tend to go it alone, as opposed to Americans, who think nothing of dragging along two or three associates.

If it were my first meeting (and first business), I would make a point of bringing along an accountant. The disadvantage of taking a male along is that it may appear you do not know what you are doing, and may even create (if the banker is male as well) a situation excluding you from the conversation and rendering you the "invisible woman." You can avoid this by throwing in a few facts and figures at appropriate times. *Please* don't simply sit and smile! Of course, an informed, prepared woman doesn't really need anyone but herself. To tell you the truth, it can depend on who is sitting on the other side of the desk.

I know of no data that suggests women are treated less favourably than men when applying for a loan, but I am aware of the reality that not all men are totally convinced that women belong in business. Maybe they're from the "old school," or perhaps they just need a good thump on the head. In any case, my experience and consultation work has taught me that forewarned is forearmed. Try to set up and establish good feelings with your lender. Who needs to fight? Use that energy to make more money.

Loan Shopping

As a result of my study on women entrepreneurs and financial institutions in western Canada, the following recommendations emerged for loan shopping:

1. *Select a lending institution that cares about small businesses*. Try to determine if the lender has knowledge of your type of business and has the time to spend with you. A lender conveniently located near your business may not necessarily be the best place for you to conduct your business.
2. *Get to know the business loans officer*. Try and find a person who knows something about your type of business and establish a rapport with him or her. Keep that person advised regularly of your progress. Use the loans officer as a sounding board — if you face a problem that will affect the financial position of the business, let it be known and seek his or her advice.

3. *You should have a good personal credit rating.* Credit card or charge accounts provide a payment history. As a woman, if you have never had a credit card in your own name, it is imperative you have one now. Your new business credit ratio will be based on your previous personal rating.
4. *Do your paperwork.* In making an application to a financial institution, use the business plan you have prepared based on the information in Chapter 4. Don't try to get by without it.
5. *Be professional in dress and demeanour.* Dress and act like a business person. Remember, businessmen wear uniform-like apparel. This doesn't mean that you need a suit, but you must be dressed for business. Casual, revealing, or dressy apparel is out; keep the look classy and understated. That means no rhinestones, sequins, tight sweaters, or open-toed shoes.
6. *Give the impression you believe in what you are doing and act confidently.* You are absolutely convinced that you and your business are winners — right?
7. *Make sure you can answer all the questions.* Take along your accountant if you feel it is necessary, but the lender will want to be satisfied you understand your business. If you don't understand the bank jargon, procedures or forms, make sure they are explained to you beforehand. If you go alone, ask at the time anything you do not understand.
8. *Borrow sufficient monies.* You should anticipate what your loan requirements will be for a year in advance, even if you don't need the funds initially.
9. *Honour your commitments.* Make your loan payments on time and have arrangements made to meet your other obligations. If you experience a financial problem discuss it with the lender, before it becomes unsolvable. By sharing the ups and downs of your business you will strengthen the business relationship with your lender.

I'd be remiss if I didn't tell you that for most people a loan to start a business is in the form of a personal rather than a business loan. The Small Business Administration SBA lends money to small-business owners below the prevailing interest rates, and lets you pay back the loan out of your profits over a long term. Your relationship with the bank must be already established. There are a number of sources for government funding in Canada, but generally do not apply to any start-up funding.

COMMON COMMERCIAL TYPES OF LENDING SOURCES IN CANADA*

Short Term	
Commercial Banks	They offer accounts receivable and inventory financing, operating loans and lines of credit, and government-guaranteed loans.
Trade Credits	Usually grant suppliers thirty to days before payment is due.
Factoring Companies	These companies buy accounts receivable outright without recourse and assume all risks of collection. Will advance funds against purchased receivables, less a percentage.
Commercial Finance Companies	These firms advance funds advanced upon assignment of receivables and warehouse receipts and offer equipment financing.
Long Term	
Commercial Banks	Commercial banks offer capital financing, funds for fixed assets and equipment, and small business development bonds.
Sales Finance Companies	These offer installment-purchase of equipment and machinery, sales of and lease-back options on equipment, and small business development bonds.
Insurance and Trust Companies	These firms make direct loans secured by a fixed asset such as a

* Independent Business Handbook, (Victoria: Province of British Columbia Ministry of Industry and Small Business Development, 1984), p. 25.

	mortgage. Also open-market loans financed by offering debt security based on the market value of your mortgage or insurance policy.
Other Term Lenders (Federal Business Development Bank, provincial business aid programs, etc.)	These agencies offer fixed-asset acquisitions, equity financing, refinancing, change of ownership services, and working capital, among others.

The Rest of Your Team

Other members of your team may include the following people:

1. An *insurance person* could and really should be utilized for a variety of reasons. One of them is illustrated in the following story.

   "One cold January morning about eight years ago, my beauty business went up in flames. The business, housed in an old sturdy red-brick building, was about as impervious to fire as any I have ever seen. The likelihood of it being gutted by fire never crossed my mind. Just one week before, I had been to see my insurance agent to secure malpractice insurance for a new employee. During that meeting, I casually inquired about the cost of fire insurance, and at the last moment *threw it in*. Need I say more? The back door of the shop had been firebombed; it was meant for the business next door. Obviously, someone had a problem counting doors!" This story illustrates why you should never say "never." Types of insurance coverage vary, as do the types of risks involved in business.

   Another scenario concerns partnerships. Suppose you own the business on a fifty-fifty basis. Fortunately, to date the relationship has worked, but what would happen if either partner were to die tomorrow? In the case of one partnership team, they drew up what is called a Shareholder's Agreement, whereby upon the death of either party, the survivor of the partnership has the right to buy out the beneficiary of the deceased partner at what is known as fair market value. In this case, where the fair market value of the business is about $1 million, one or the other might be hard pressed to come up with immediate financing. To cover this eventuality, partners can each independently hold an insurance policy for half a million dollars on the life of the other. Make use of a reputable tax consultant and an insurance professional for this type of advice. You should remember to update your insurance needs as your company grows.

You will want to consider business interruption insurance, key person or income replacement, theft, medical, shareholders or partners, and a raft of others. Make sure your insurance person understands the nature of your business so the best possible advice can be rendered. Only you and your insurance professional can decide exactly what you and your business need. Consider all the options. Shop and compare!

2. A *business consultant* may well be part of your team. First of all, let's clarify what this term means. These days you can find a consultant in just about everything from office automation to dog psychology. These are all people whose opinion or advice in a specific area is available for a fee. A consultant is an independent contractor, usually self-employed, who is willing and able to perform a specific task. Will you need a consultant in your business?

   You have every right to ask about the backgrounds, education, and business qualifications of these people. Make sure they are familiar with your type of business or, at least, that they understand the problem facing you. A business consultant is often used to determine why a company is having problems in specific areas. As a new business, you may want to use one for guidance in inventory, pricing, and general business advice. The consulting business has grown by leaps and bounds over the last ten years, and is now one of the major service areas in North America. Among the causes are the major layoffs and cutbacks in large industries and corporations in both Canada and the United States. The marketplace is flooded with individuals with tremendous knowledge and experience who are able to offer expertise on a fee-for-service basis. Lucky you.

3. A good *market consultant* can help you get those tickets sold and the bleachers filled. In other words, marketing fulfills a

need, real or imagined, at a price people are willing to pay. Therefore, your market becomes those people who need your product, are in a position to purchase it, and are willing to pay for it. Whether it's a product or service, nothing happens without marketing. A good marketing consultant can analyze your situation and determine the problems and opportunities. You may feel you have a better mousetrap, but until the marketplace agrees and is willing to buy, nary a nickel can be made.

4. *Computer consultants,* both generalists and specialists, can save you time and money. They can define your needs, help set priorities, select the right combination of equipment, and establish softwear or services perhaps all within your budget. The most important decision they can make for you is whether or not your business would benefit from a computer in the first place.

   Buying a computer with limited knowledge is a little like going to the refreshment stand blindfolded and pointing. Even though you may not need a computer at this stage, you will probably be making some office equipment purchases. It's possible that the equipment you select will be influenced to some degree by the opinion and advice of a computer consultant.

5. *Professional business clubs* and associations are really your cheerleaders. They're highly visible and exist to encourage enthusiastic support of their members. Recognize them as a needed and active part of your support system. The relationship between small business and professional clubs and associations is a reciprocal one. That initial contact at a club or association meeting usually starts out as an information session but quickly turns into new business, and often into friendships as well.

   Determine which associations and clubs would most benefit you. Certainly any professional club in your field of endeavour, women's business and professional clubs, women's networks, and Chambers of Commerce will all be of value in some way. A word of caution here: don't restrict yourself to clubs for women only. Men have been at the game of business for a long time. I guarantee that there will be some who will appreciate your strength and courage in starting a business, and will feel good about helping you along.

There is something else men can teach us about business — it's called networking. Because business has so long been a male domain, men have accumulated contacts and relationships that support their endeavour. One of the problems women seem to have in acquiring business contacts is that they do not understand that, while club activities are for relaxation and enjoyment, they have another major function — to generate new business. Women who have learned to genuinely like and respect and share with each other, on a professional as well as personal basis, also generate business in this way.

6. *Family and friends* will provide the support to help you keep going. The pressures of going into business are numerous and will take all the ongoing support and encouragement you can muster.

   One great way of getting the support of your children is to involve them in your business. I know of many women who have their kids delivering flyers, typing invoices, or scanning papers for competition. An added bonus to this sharing is that whatever you pay them as helpers is a legitimate business expense.

7. And finally, team players you won't always see acknowledged as such are your *employees*. You may not be in a position to hire initially, but when you do, keep your emotions for those you don't hire. Hire on the basis of what your employees can do for your company. After you have been able to determine the tasks required to operate your business, the skill required to perform them, and the areas of responsibility that need filling, hire the right person. You have every right to expect that person to be a team player. Sometimes this fact may have to be spelled out; sometimes you may have to sweeten the pot with benefits, or profit-sharing, or medical coverage. Keep in mind that employees who do not play with you ultimately play against you.

Chapter 8

PARTNERSHIPS: A MARRIAGE OF BUSINESS

Why not? If you are prepared to give up a part of your life, do it. With a partner you can spread the responsibility around a little more.

Marion LaVigne,
Partner, Outcrop Ltd.

If it works for Marion LaVigne and her partner Ronne Heming in the Northwest Territories, could there be a chance for you and a partner in Canada's south, east, or west? Maybe. While LaVigne was working as head of tourism promotion for the government of the Northwest Territories after a stint in corporate communications in Toronto, Heming was busy doing audio-visual presentations for Alcan. Together they have managed to take Outcrop, the Northwest Territories' only advertising agency, from a one-room operation with revenues of $7,000 ten years ago, to billings of $1.85 million in 1985. In the beginning, Outcrop did just about anything the client wanted: public relations, advertising, typesetting, graphics, consulting, audio-visual presentations. Today, it's different. They have not only streamlined their operation and become magazine publishers (*Up Here*, launched in 1984) but have also cut back on their initial attempt to publish a second magazine, *Business North*, despite a federal-territorial Economic Development Agreement start-up grant of $94,000. At the time, Outcrop was undercapitalized, but through a beefed-up southern marketing scheme for *Up Here*, LaVigne feels they are on safe ground. Their combined experience in the audio-visual field has not gone to waste: in ten native languages, they're marketing a straightforward message to the people from the government.

Looking for a partner? Then sit down and write your business and personal goals on a piece of paper and have your prospective partner do the same. It's a method used by marriage counsellors, and when you think of it, a business partnership is not very different from a marriage. The idea of having someone to bounce your ideas off, to share the responsibility and pressure of month-end, and to cooperate in achieving your business goals can be financially rewarding as well as emotionally gratifying.

Unfortunately, with all this good news comes the reality that the potential for failure is about as great for business partners as for any marriage — complete with disenchantment, broken dreams, and the messy clean-up after things fall apart. Author Jeanette Scollard, in her book *The Self-Employed Woman,* cautions, "For almost everyone, a partnership should be a last resort." It is a difficult relationship, but no riskier than marriage. As one young entrepreneur explained, "It was lonely and difficult on my own at first. Even now — my business is graphic design — I feel pressured by being solely responsible for deadlines. I should have considered a partnership to offset the workload and expenses."

The key in the selection process for finding a business partner is to avoid the Just-Like-Me trap. While the relationship may feel comfortable, you are staring at a potential disaster in disguise. Find someone who complements your business skills rather than duplicating them. I know of one partnership where two women pooled their business experience, tallying almost fifty years of combined legal expertise. Where can you buy that kind of experience? The partnership evolved from a friendship spanning six years. Generally, friends probably should not go into business together, but these two had talked about a joint venture so many times in the past that, when an offer to bankroll the venture was made, they decided to make the plunge. Today, L & L Legal Typing Services "for the lawyer and the layman" has all partners happy. Joyce Grandison and Glory Ewen combine Ewen's para-legal background with Grandison's notary-public expertise to position them as a complete legal service. "Not only that," says Grandison, "we were practising in the fifties, before lawyers started specializing. We worked on everything from conveyancing to insurance." Their business and their friendship are both intact.

A Quiz for Potential Partners

If you do have someone in mind for a partnership and you happen to be friends, protect that friendship first by jointly working through the following questions.

1. *Do we understand which business skills each of us brings to the enterprise?* There is absolutely no reason why one computer consultant should team up with another. You should be looking for someone who can run the business while you are drumming up more. Preferably, you should be looking for someone who at least understands and cares about the world of computers.
2. *Do we have the same business goals in mind?* What happens if your friend wants to go into business to make a living, and your goal is to gain control of a particular market?

3. *Do we share the same level of commitment to the enterprise?* There you are, your business is six months old, and seven days a week you're bookkeeping, filing, writing reports and letters, returning calls, and promoting the business. Your partner, whom you've known since you were in your teens, is terrific — when she works. Somehow she finds no necessity to work after 5:00 p.m. nor even one day on the weekend. This is not unusual.
4. *Do we have compatible work habits?* Some people are neat freaks and others claim they work best when debris surrounds them. If you don't have separate work areas, you've got a problem. The lover of debris will see to it that the stapler, files, and maybe even the telephone cannot be found at the snap of a finger. For some, simply seeing chaos is enough to make them feel uneasy — never mind working in it day after day.
5. *Do we have the same priorities?* It may well be that you are single and your would-be partner is married with school age children. Those times when she is away on family business may, over a period of time, leave you weary. There may be good reasons for her absenteeism, but if you have already acquired a businesslike attitude, you may resent her not being there. This is a sticky one, in that trust and fairness will play a large role in keeping this problem under wraps.
6. *Do we both project the same image to the community?* It is important to consider the type of operation you are running when deciding on an appropriate image as well as on a partner. What if you are thinking of forming a public relations company? You project what's called an "uptown" image, and your very knowledgeable friend presents a real "down-home" image visually, and every time she opens her mouth. As a friend, you find it refreshing, but you'd better take a look at how she would be judged by the business community. Or maybe it is a preventive medicine clinic you want to launch: you project a very caring image, while it is obvious that only the bottom line counts for your would-be partner.

Needless to say, this quiz should also be used as a guideline for someone who is not your friend. In addition, for such people you will have to do some serious checking. You need to know who they are, where they come from, and whether they are a good risk. Can they be trusted? Regardless of who your partner is, you should spell out exactly what your individual job definitions and responsibilities are. Include everything from banking to sweeping the floor.

Why a Partnership? Pros and Cons

There are several reasons why people consider partnerships. For starters, the major advantage of any partnership over a sole proprietorship is the advantage of more capital. If several people go into business together, they may create not only the opportunity for more capital, but also the opportunity for diversification. Individual partners may have specific talents that would contribute to the business's scope. Financing may also be easier to arrange. The lender would have the assets of several people as collateral. This may also prove to be an advantage when dealing with suppliers. And, let's face it, not everyone is cut out to run a business independently. Many an entrepreneur has failed, not because of a lack of a salable product, service, or commodity, but because of a lack of sufficient management skills. And lastly, the amount of motivation and energy needed to keep a sole proprietorship floating can be exhausting. Doubling the members of the firm also doubles the spirit of enterprise.

But as in any marriage, there are downsides to contend with. In Chapter 7 you learned that in a sole proprietorship you are responsible for the debts of your business. This is what also happens in a partnership, but to make matters worse, you are also responsible for the debts accrued by your business partner on behalf of the business. This creates the possibility that both partners' personal assets could be up for grabs should debts remain outstanding and the business simply not be able to cover them. Another real disadvantage to a partnership is the reality that you are making an agreement with one or more individuals; make any change to that arrangement, add or subtract players, and the status of your company is no longer in place. It calls for a new partnership agreement. So be sure your partnership agreement includes a first option to buy out your original partner(s). What's more, conflicting managerial styles can be enough to end an agreement. What if one partner believes power comes from the top and one believes in grassroots management? Lastly, the chances of pulling your money out of the partnership in a hurry are slim; it may involve costly and time-consuming legal and administrative procedures.

Why Partnerships Fail

In *The Self-Employed Woman*, Jeanette Scollard lists twenty-five reasons why partnerships fail:

1. Partner brought in solely to raise money.
2. Partner brought in solely to perform one service and performs unsatisfactorily.
3. Overlapping responsibilities.
4. Different concepts of company's direction.
5. Different concepts about spending money.
6. One person feels she or he is doing all the work.
7. One person goofs off.
8. Personality clashes.
9. Different life or management styles.
10. Different philosophies of how business should be run.
11. Different ambitions.
12. Unwillingness to share credit.
13. Competition between the partners: ego clashes.
14. Disagreements over money being spent.
15. Disagreements over rate of growth.
16. Disagreements over direction of growth.
17. Greed.
18. One partner shifts priorities and goals.
19. One partner loses ambition.
20. Spouse conflict: interfering relatives.
21. Difficulties in the business: partners blame each other.
22. One partner feels the other hinders the company's progress.
23. One partner fails to produce as promised.
24. People's tolerance of change is different.
25. People change.

A Partnership Contract

One of the ways you can help protect yourself from these pitfalls is to draw up a contract. Make sure you do it while you still have total trust and belief in each other. In it include the worst possible scenarios: the death of your partner; the appearance of an investor who wants to buy out one or both of you; one or both of you want to sell; one of you is hit by a car and is seriously disabled for an extended period of time. I've talked with several women contemplating forming partnerships and have found that it is not too unusual for women to seriously question the need for such a document. Think of it as insurance. You may never need it, but it's your best hedge against the unexpected. Some contracts include job responsibilities and details such as cheque-signing authority, as well as any other clause that is essential to the longevity or dissolution of the venture.

Robert Katz, a partner in Arthur Anderson & Co., Chartered Accountants, wrote for the *B.C. Industry and Small Business News*, "An effective partnership agreement devised in consultation with a lawyer and accountant should cover the following basic areas: the contribution of the partners (who puts in what, including cash, know-how, office furniture); the division of duties (which partner does what); the division of profits and losses (sharing the spoils); family matters." Family matters include provisions for admitting new partners, for arbitrating policy disagreements, for changing operating directions (e.g., diversifying, slowing down), and for handling the departure of a partner for whatever reason. These matters, says Katz, "almost never get adequate attention."

Douglas Gray, a Vancouver lawyer and author of *The Entrepreneur's Complete Self-Assessment Guide*, offers the following checklist for a partnership agreement:

1. Name, purpose, and location of partnership
2. Duration of agreement
3. Names and categories of partners
4. Financial contribution by partners
5. Role of individual partners in business management
6. Authority of partner in conduct of business
7. Nature and degree of each partner's contribution to the business

8. How business expenses will be handled
9. Separate debts
10. Signing of checks
11. Division of profits and losses
12. Books, records, and method of accounting
13. Draws or salaries
14. Absence and disability
15. Death of a partner (dissolution and winding up)
16. Rights of the continuing partner
17. Employee management
18. Sale of partnership interest
19. Release of debts
20. Settlement of disputes and arbitration
21. Additions, alterations, or modifications to partnership agreement
22. Non-competition in the event of departure

The Nuts and Bolts of Partnerships

Below are the legal aspects of partnerships that you should be familiar with.

A partnership is a legal entity. Partners, according to the law, are generally classified as working or silent, general or limited. A silent partner provides only money; a working partner provides both money and skills and is involved in the day-to-day operation of the business. A general partner has unlimited liability for all debts and obligations of the partnership; a limited partner is not responsible for the business's debts and obligations. As a general warning, if you need capital, try to find another way to get it other than bringing in a partner. At the very least, don't take on a partner for this reason without very close scrutiny.

1. Legal costs are minimal, if only the registration of the partnership and a licence to operate is required. If a lawyer is hired to draw up a partnership agreement, fees will vary; solicit quotations.
2. Legal regulations are minimal.
3. Decisions concerning business operations may or may not be mutually decided upon by partners. Spell out this authority structure in your agreement. All partners are legally bound

by the action of the others. Partnership disagreements may interfere with the operations of the company.
4. Capital is increased by pooling financial resources and personal assets from partners. This makes borrowing, if necessary, less difficult.
5. The profits of the business are distributed to the partners in accordance with a pre-determined sharing ratio.
6. Business profits are split among partners in accordance with their sharing ratio, and partners file personal tax returns on their specified income.
7. Your liability is unlimited. All general partners are personally responsible for the debts and obligations of the business, and their personal assets are subject to claim. This holds true for debts and obligations incurred with and without mutual agreement of all partners.
8. The business may be discontinued if one partner dies or wants to withdraw. Provisions for dealing with this may be covered in a partnership agreement.
9. Since the decision to shut down may not be mutual, provision to deal with this possibility should be in a partnership agreement.

(Adapted from *Legal Structures of a Small Business: Management Clinic Workbook No.4*, issued by the Federal Business Development Bank.)

Finding a Partner — Creative Alternatives

Keep in mind that friends or working associates may not be the only potential business partners. Your family may be an excellent source. At least you will know each other's personalities and perhaps have some appreciation of the lifestyle and business needs of each other. Again, it may not work out simply because of the comfort level — it would be pretty difficult to fire or end an agreement with your mother-in-law. On the other hand, many Canadian women are in business with their husbands. A good husband-and-wife team provides an excellent ongoing team commitment that may prove stronger than in other combinations. However, too much of a good thing — overexposure to one's spouse — may be a little more than one or the other can handle.

Don't overlook the classified ads. People with money to invest or the talent to contribute are frequently looking for business opportunities. But do not forget to do your homework and check them out thoroughly before any commitment is made.

Another way to get into partnering is to form associations with other entrepreneurs. Frequently, large offices are rented by a group of people and costs are shared. One of the services of L & L Legal Typing Services is the rental of office space with full secretarial services. It is not only cost-effective but creates a warm environment for those tired of the solitary feeling of working alone.

One business owner had this to say about her partnership: "I would do more thinking about partnerships. I am not complaining about my partners, but about what we got ourselves into. We did not anticipate problems even in a general way. We did not (and still don't have) a decision-making method, other than exerting our own personalities, which wastes energy. Because of the nature of our work, we often work closely with each other. Organizing work flow — accounting for each other's strengths, weaknesses, interests, work habits — can be exhausting. None of this is bad, but we just weren't prepared for it. And in my mind at least, preparedness helps one adapt faster!"

Chapter 9

THE FRANCHISE CONNECTION

Franchise sales could top $2.5 trillion by the year 2010.

John Naisbitt,
Author of *Megatrends*

John Naisbitt's latest forecast heralds an extremely bright future for franchising. In *The Future of Franchising: Looking 25 Years Ahead to the Year 2010*, commissioned by the International Franchise Association and written by Naisbitt, he highlights the top ten franchise industries in the following chart:

GROWTH OF TOP FORMAT FRANCHISE INDUSTRIES, 1985-1990

Business	Annual Sales (in billions) 1985	1990	% Growth
Restaurants (All Types)	$ 48.9	$ 86.1	12.0
Retailing (Nonfood)	18.8	33.6	12.3
Hotels, Motels, Campgrounds	14.6	22.5	9.0
Convenience Stores	12.3	19.4	9.5
Business Aids and Services	12.1	21.3	12.0
Automotive Products and Services	10.6	15.9	8.5
Retailing (Food other than convenience stores)	10.2	15.9	7.0
Rental Services (Auto, Truck)	5.3	8.9	11.0
Construction and Home Services	3.7	9.25	20.0
Recreation, Entertainment, Travel	1.8	6.6	29.0
TOTAL TOP TEN	$138.5	$238.1	11.5

The term *franchising* covers many different types of business arrangements. The Association of Canadian Franchisors defines it as "an ongoing contractual agreement between two parties, franchisor and franchisee." Franchisors grant the right to market a product or service, including the use of a trademark. They also provide a tested format or system, as well as know-how in a wide variety of areas. Franchisees are expected to conform to the format, maintain quality standards, and pay a set fee for the franchise.

The concept of franchising is not new; it dates back for centuries. But it was the Singer Sewing Machine Company that gave franchising its modern form about one hundred years ago. Today, people generally buy what is known as a *business format franchise*. It may take the form of a turn-key operation, in that it allows the franchisee to do just that — turn the key and the door opens to an instant business. Or it may be sold in a straight "packaged" format in which certain variables such as location are not provided. For a certain amount of money, the franchisor will provide to the franchisee (conditions and agreements may vary) assistance in obtaining financing, site selection/evaluation and acquisition, construction and equipping of premises, training of the franchisee and his or her staff, provision of start-up assistance, purchasing assistance for inventory, provision of management and accounting systems, provision of advertising, publicity, and marketing services, and ongoing supervision and guidance of the business.

Franchisors such as Molly Maid, Colours, Cookies by George, Kettle Creek Canvas Co., The Flag Shop, Proper Nails, Inc., and Fantastic Sam's (and I'm sure there are other wonderful ones) have done all the groundwork for you, so the relationship is simple. When you succeed, they succeed. On the other hand, if they go out of business, so do you. For now, let us look at this relationship in the best possible light. You are a potential franchisee with about $12,000 to invest in some kind of business. You've got a few ideas of your own, but all the start-up costs and hassles simply are not appealing. A franchise may be your best option. Such was the case for 23-year-old Molly Maid franchisee, Lenore Schur, who thought to herself, "Hey, that's a possibility for me to start something in the future." The future came, and despite the initially mixed feelings of her father (he has since turned very supportive), Schur knew she was not the kind of person who could start a business from scratch. "I find that if I run across a problem that I don't know how to deal with, I have someone to turn to."

Another franchisee I talked with was older and more sophisticated; in contrast to Schur's three teams of cleaning ladies, she had five teams of two each. (As a Molly Maid franchisee, you do not necessarily do the cleaning yourself; you hire teams of women who you feel will go out and do a good job for you.)

Linda Hodgson (who happens to be Molly Maid founder Adrienne Stringer's sister-in-law) did not want to go through the hassles of starting a business, either. She was not sure what to do, but what she did know was that she wanted to work out of her home. "People choose us for three reasons," says Hodgson. "We're professional, the price is right, and they can make a personal decision on who they would like to deal with." A whole lot of people must like dealing with her, since her business brings in about $275,000 a year.

Not all franchises will provide you with that level of success. So where do you start? Just as you interviewed a number of successful women entrepreneurs in Chapter 1, so you should follow the same process when considering a franchise. I am not talking about one or two or three: I'm suggesting you talk with every franchisor who interests you, and who requires an investment you can afford. Owning a franchise allows you the independence of being in business, with the ability to short-circuit many of the management requirements of other entrepreneurial pursuits.

Says F.A. (Al) Droppo, president of the Canadian Bankers' Association, "I believe the most important reason for the success of franchisees revolves around the degree of expertise provided by franchisors in those areas where typical entrepreneurs are not particularly experienced — that is business planning, financial reporting and monitoring, market research, and advertising. Good franchisors assist in these areas and insist on their implementation."

"Women are interested and extremely capable of operating their own business, especially franchising; it's their best opportunity for success," writes Connie Boling in *The Franchise Handbook*. The quote comes from a division manager for an Indiana-based franchise, but it could have come from anyone. One such person is the president of Molly Maid, James MacKenzie, who feels that women are better managers than men. The Molly Maid success story is one worth heeding. Their expansion into the United Kingdom, the United States, and soon into Australia, makes them the largest homecare cleaning franchise in the world. "Either by design or happenstance," says MacKenzie, "McDonald's was our role model. Those who are just starting in the homecare business are now using us for theirs." Why franchising? Adrienne Stringer wanted her company to grow and knew it was conducive to franchising because, "it is the kind of business you manage in a small, isolated area. You maintain control. It thrives on close management in areas with a very dense population."

While these may be some of the reasons for selling a franchise, why would anyone want to buy one? Consider the case of Nancy Cameron, a Halifax franchisee of a company called Colours. In 1980, with $10,000, Cameron bought herself an opportunity for employment. "I really wanted to create something on my own. I'd been a teacher, and successful at it," says Cameron, "but needed to have that sense of control." Today, she spends three or four months a year vacationing in Florida. I could be wrong, but in all probability a Halifax schoolteacher's salary would be a far cry from Cameron's $400,000 yearly volume of business. While not all franchises guarantee huge profits, some of the sellers are becoming multi-millionaires, and buyers are playing in a league they, too, never before dreamed possible.

As if this were not exciting enough, John Naisbitt says that, "by the year 2000 almost any service imaginable will be franchised."I don't know about you, but I personally have no great need to doubt John Naisbitt. And there are other reasons to become a part of the franchising trend. According to John Gillespie, president of the Association of Canadian Franchisors, in a special "Report on Franchising" in the *Globe and Mail*, "It's part of the fallout from the early 1980s. People discovered that traditional job security just isn't there any more and they started to look more and more at getting into business themselves. With a franchise, you can be your own boss, but you're not completely on your own; you get a success formula and a proven track record that helps you get through those very difficult first three years when most businesses fail." For some, franchising is an obvious solution to job independence where job expertise may be missing.

"In 1985," according to the same report, "there were 1,200 different franchise systems in Canada with 50,000 franchise outlets." Sales are projected to top $50 billion this year. Not only that, they are expected to increase 50 per cent by 1990, with about 150,000 new jobs a year created in the process, according to the International Franchise Association. There is a "surge in entrepreneurial spirit,'' and the business of franchising ''is looking ahead to unprecedented growth for the rest of the decade.''

How is it being done? How do you know if you should be a franchisor or a franchisee? There is probably no single answer. But you may be assured that those who do get involved have paid attention to trends, used their instincts, and hired the best advice money can buy.

Buying a Franchise or Starting from Scratch

First, let's take a look at franchising from the standpoint of the franchisee. Words of caution come from Al Droppo, president of the Canadian Bankers' Association. ''Realistically consider the input resources required of yourself and your family in both financial and personal terms.'' Once you have selected a potential franchise, ''talk with a few of the already existing franchise holders about their experiences.'' As a franchisee, you may have a better chance of success than if you had started from scratch (the Association of Canadian Franchisors is boasting a 90 per cent success rate) but be warned: ''just because you're buying a franchise it doesn't mean you don't have to do your homework,'' according to one Royal Bank manager for Independent Business, Brian Hann.

Let's take a look at some of the most important factors. The following characteristics of life as a franchise owner versus those of someone who has started her own business are adapted from *Buying a Franchise*, published by the Federal Business Development Bank.

When You Buy a Franchise:

1. Operational training is usually provided by franchisor.
2. You have the right to use a known trade name or trademark. Franchise operation is completely identified with the franchisor.
3. You are able to see a proven product or service with established public acceptance.
4. You are buying a package, so are ready to start full operations sooner.
5. You may require less working capital because of tighter controls and franchisor's terms of merchandise supply.

6. Your profit-and-loss forecasts may be more accurate, based on proven similar operations.
7. You have greater chance of initial success.
8. Your sales territory is defined by the franchisor.
9. You benefit from standard national and local advertising of prices, products, and service.
10. The franchisor is often the sole source for merchandise.
11. Fixtures, equipment, and premises are often specified by franchisor.
12. Your contractual arrangement covers all aspects of operation and duration of franchisee's right to operate the franchise.

When You Start Your Own Business:

1. Your management ability is based on your own expertise.
2. Time is required to establish name, but there is a closer identification of owner and business.
3. It takes time to establish your business presence.
4. You may have to start more slowly and take a longer time to realize full potential.
5. Risk of mistakes and longer time to start can mean greater financing needs. Terms may be difficult to get with suppliers.
6. You risk making serious errors in estimating expenses, sales, and profits, especially for an unproven venture.
7. There is a great chance of failure because of the time required for establishment and the possibility of mistakes, especially in marketing and planning.
8. There are no restrictions on expanding your territory if successful, and no risks that expanded territory already has operations identical to yours.
9. You have the freedom to advertise when you want to and can afford to, as well as the ability to set your own specials and discounts to meet competition.
10. You can buy from any supplier in order to get the best prices and terms.
11. You decide on premises, equipment, and fixtures based on the image you want and available capital.
12. You have total freedom to operate as you see fit and to sell or close the business when you want.

Choosing the Right Franchise

Whether or not it sounds like a "good deal," be sure you really love the industry and you have done your homework. Adeline Wieb bought the exclusive Canadian rights to "the original family haircutters," Fantastic Sam's. What she became was a *subfranchisor*. But, before she purchased from her franchisor, her franchise shopping went something like this. She discovered there were 150 hair franchises in the U.S. Wieb, a former successful salon owner and real estate broker, decided that the combination of her two professions would be ideal. She worked through that list of 150 potentials and knocked it down to fifty, then personally checked out twenty-five, dropping another twenty-five from the selection, then reducing the number to ten. By the time she was down to three, she sat on their doorsteps for a week at a time. She discovered which ones had clients. Then she bought.

That careful shopping has paid off. She sold rights first to British Columbia, then Ontario. By the time the Maritimes deal is closed, she will have sold off her rights to Fantastic Sam's in every province. A $3.5-million offer for her business was turned down in 1985; one can only guess what the lady would settle for today.

Approach the purchasing of a franchise with the same critical self-assessment you would undertake if you were starting your business from scratch. Association of Canadian Franchisors president John Gillespie, who is also president of the franchise Pizza-Pizza, gives prospective franchisees in his set-up the opportunity to back out of the agreement before the end of the training period. One franchisee discovered she did not like making pizzas!

Your library or a large branch of any one of the major five banking institutions will have a copy of *The 1986 Franchise Annual*, which lists all franchises in Canada, the U.S., and elsewhere. You may also try major newspapers as a source of potential franchisors. But be wary. Here are two beauts from advertisements in a Vancouver newspaper:

> *Gift (Jewelry, Brass, etc.) Franchise stores*, fully set up with inventory & displays. Starting at $16,000. Profits after expenses, $5-7,000 per month. Backed by importer.

> *Now franchising*. Proven system showing good profits. Low investment. Complete set-up and training.

Let's examine them one at a time. In the first, do not be impressed by an advertisement assuring you of profits after expenses. No one can guarantee profits. Because it would be your business, if you chose not to work, you could not expect profits. One banker I know observed a franchisee buy a business and stand around waiting for customers to walk in the door. Furthermore, this advertisement says nothing about training, nor does it even give the name of the company. I can just imagine the person who placed this advertisement responding to an inquiry, saying, "Look, lady, there are only two franchises left, but if you come in today with your money, I can hold it for you — but just today." Don't laugh; they do it to men, too.

The next advertisement really irks me because of its lack of specifics. About the only credible thing going for the company is that it has some kind of "set-up" (whatever that is) and training. This is not to say that all small ads promoting franchises are losers. There are a number of things you should do in order to assess the viability of an advertised franchise. First and foremost, call the number in the advertisement and then pay them a visit. Once you have established that a company actually exists, start playing detective. Find out how long they have been in business, and get the names and addresses of three people holding a franchise with them, two well-established and one new (established less than six months). Go and talk with the franchisees. That way, you will be getting a good reading on the reality of the profits (after royalties, usually 2 to 9 per cent) as well as franchisor performance in terms of training and management support.

Consider what one banker called the "franchise enchantment cycle." There seems to be a real love/hate relationship between the franchisee and franchisor, in some cases. There's definitely a cycle. At first, there is a heavy dependency on the franchisor: it lasts about six months. After about eighteen months, negativity begins to set in. The question then asked by franchisees is, "Why should I continue to pay my royalty?"

Brian Hann of the Royal Bank, gives this advice when considering a potential franchisor:

1. Approach a valid franchise. A good franchisor is more interested in the long-term survival of the franchise than the

quick-buck franchising fee. Look for a franchise that's been around about three years, with some kind of proven track record.

2. Look for depth in management. Can they help you with management? Are they providing supervisory and accounting support? Will they be providing the advertising back-up?
3. Financial stability is a must. If the franchisor goes broke, so do you. Have a look at their financial statements. If they won't show you, don't do business with them.

Don't stop there. You'll need to contact your Better Business Bureau, which in turn has access to the Canadian Council of Better Business Bureaus. According to Paul Tuz, president of the Council, "the BBB records all complaints they receive about member and non-member businesses, including complaints by franchisees. In the cases of some franchises, the files bulge."

Contact Consumer and Corporate Affairs, the Association of Canadian Franchisors, and your city hall in regard to planning and zoning regulations. One woman bought a franchise in a large metropolitan city on a major thoroughfare. Shortly thereafter, the city came along and started digging up the street. For two and a half weeks this newly opened franchise not only had no road traffic, but no pedestrian traffic, either. After completion of the work, the city erected No Parking signs up and down the street — right in front of her business. There the story ends. She went broke.

A *Small Business* article by Michael Crawford outlines some of the important initial questions to ask a franchisor:

What is your own personal business experience?
Did this business start out as a franchise or as an independent business?
How long was this business operating before you started franchising it?
How many franchises are there and where are they?
Have all of your franchisees been successful? If not, why?
How many other new franchises are opening?
What are your long-range expansion plans?

You should be hearing that the franchisor has business experience, that the business started out as an independent business, and that the business has been operating successfully for about three years. Numbers and locations of franchises should be offered without a stutter. Listen carefully if they try to explain away the fact that a franchise has gone belly-up. Could it be that the franchisee was not properly trained or screened initially? If you smell a big turnover in franchisees, run — do not walk — to an alternative franchisor. Finally, long-range plans for expansion had better include you.

Once you've assessed a franchisor's credibility, you will want to know its credit rating. According to the Association of Canadian Franchisors, "any reputable franchisor should give you full financial information, such as past financial performance records of franchisees, required investment capital, and the related costs of operating the franchise." What you should know is that generally, privately incorporated franchises operating only in Canada are not legally required to disclose any extensive financial or corporate information, except in the province of Alberta. It's a little easier to get information on those offering public shares, as they would be registered through the securities commission of the province where the shares are being offered. This kind of financial disclosure is mandatory if a franchise operates in the U.S., where franchises are subject to United States laws and the U.S. Federal Trade Commission.

You are going to need some strong team players in this game. The franchise connection calls for an accountant, a banker, and a lawyer, preferably one specializing in franchising. This is no time for skimping. Says franchise expert Jerry White, of the Toronto consulting firm Laventhol & Horwath, "Hire a franchise consultant or franchise lawyer to check out the company. If you can't afford to hire at least a qualified chartered accountant you probably shouldn't be going into business." White adds, "Some people will take a mortgage on their house and put up everything they own, but won't spend $3,000 on a professional to get a proper business plan."

Frank Zaid, a franchising lawyer with the Toronto firm Osler, Hoskins & Harcourt, has this to say, "First the potential franchisee[s] must recognize that they need expert advice. The most important question they should ask is, 'What is your experience? Give me references.' If their lawyer is honest and does not have that kind of expertise, they can work through that lawyer to retain someone else who does, or they can retain someone independently. I've seen so many instances (and so many of our clients are people who have used inexperienced advisors and are now trying to redo a franchise agreement) where it has proven to be extremely costly and difficult. There is a great deal of business understanding that should go into advising someone when they are buying a franchise . . . [inexperienced lawyers may] pick up some of the pure legal points and . . . . miss a lot of the business aspects that are key for the protection of the franchisee or franchisor. The other thing is that franchising is a rapidly evolving field of law, a new field, and to really have a full understanding of things that are likely to develop you have to keep yourself informed of recent cases, of legislative developments, and probably most importantly the trends in the United States, because they tend to influence the direction of the legal aspects of franchising. If a lawyer is not committed to that kind of ongoing education, you can really get hit-and-miss advice."

Franchise Evaluation Checklist

You may want to use the following franchise evaluation checklist, adapted from a list published by the Federal Business Development Bank, when contemplating buying a franchise. Note how similar some of these questions are to those you have already asked yourself with regard to entrepreneurship in general.

Evaluation of a franchisee	Yes	No
Do you know why you want to buy a franchise?		
Are you interested in working in the franchise you have chosen?		
Do you have the physical, work-related/educational requirements to make the franchise succeed?		
Do you have good learning abilities and the willingness to work hard?		
Are you prepared for the financial risk?		
Can you manage staff?		
Can you work under the rules, controls, and regulations specified by the franchisor?		

Evaluation of a franchisor	Yes	No
Do you know who the principals are?		
Do you know their personal and business history as it relates to the franchise?		
Was the business originally set up as a franchise? If not, after what period of time did it become one?		
Evaluation of the franchise operation		
Is the franchise operation well established?		
Is it a growing business with an indicated good future?		
Do you know what the franchisor owns or controls (trade name, trademark, product, process)?		
Have you been given the names and addresses of other established franchisees?		
Have you visited and talked with these as well as others?		
Evaluation of sales and profit		
Have you estimated sales, expenses, and profit, and made a point of comparing them to an existing franchise?		
Has a professional accountant helped you?		
Have you studied the market?		
Have you assessed your share of the market?		
Evaluation of location and premises		
Can you choose your location?		
Is your location the best one for you?		
Are there standards for location and premises specified by the franchisor?		
Do you know if you must lease or buy your premises? If so, have you checked the terms?		
Evaluation of equipment, fixtures, and layout		
Are the equipment and fixtures specified?		
Must you buy or lease the specific equipment and fixtures only from the franchisor?		

	Yes	No
If so, are the terms and prices reasonable compared to other sources?		
Is the layout specified by the franchisor?		
Can you make adaptations to the layout?		
Evaluation of the protection of your territory		
Is your territory well defined?		
Do you know how your territory is protected?		
Can your territory be reduced or expanded?		
Evaluation of purchase costs		
Do you know what the franchise fee entitles you to?		
Is the franchise fee a one-time payment?		
Have you checked for royalties and service charges?		
Do you know who pays for the legal fees, permits, licences, and insurance?		
Have you made financial arrangements for equipment and premises?		
Can you arrange financing with the franchisor?		
Evaluation of Training		
Will the franchisor train you and your staff?		
If so, do you know who pays for this?		
Evaluation of prices and sales		
Are the prices set by the franchisor?		
Can you adjust the prices or offer special discounts?		
Are there sales quotas and are they realistic?		
Do you know what happens if you don't reach the quotas?		
Evaluation of products and supplies		
Must you carry all the franchisor's product lines?		

	Yes	No
Can you stock product lines other than the franchisor's?		
Is the source for products and supplies specified?		
Can you arrange terms for the products and supplies?		
Evaluation of business controls		
Has the franchisor specified rules and regulations in running your franchise?		
Do you know what all the rules and regulations are?		
Are you in agreement with them?		
Can these rules and regulations be adjusted?		
Evaluation of the franchise agreement		
Do you understand all clauses of the contract? Is everything that you want written in the document?		
Have you especially checked the conditions of termination, bankruptcy, transfer, renewal, and sale?		
Has your lawyer read each clause and explained them all to you?		

Remember that there are two kinds of franchises: the *packaged franchise*, such as a fast-food outlet, where a franchisee is licensed to do business under a prepared business format, under which you will use the franchisor's trademark; and the *product franchise*, used by car dealerships and other vendors, where the franchisee is simply a distributor of goods bearing the franchisor's trademark and produced by or on behalf of the franchisor.

The Franchise Agreement

Toronto franchising lawyer Frank Zaid, author of *The Canadian Franchise Guide*, warns that

> there are several typical areas where franchisees tend to develop negative attitudes over a period of time. First, the franchisees tend to think over a time that they are not

> getting the benefit of good advertising for the advertising contribution they are making. A second area of common concern is that of purchasing supplies. There are rigid requirements for the purchasing of products and designated suppliers. The important thing in many of these areas is disclosure and reasonableness. In the product purchasing area, if the franchisor had disclosed to the franchisee the extent to which there are going to be any profits or rebates, there shouldn't be any cause for concern as long as the price and the terms of supply that the franchisee has are reasonable. Frequently it is not spelled out in the franchise agreement, because franchisors are not well advised that they should put this in an agreement or franchisees are not advised that they should ask the question. The third area is rebates. Are they going to be passed on to the franchisor from suppliers, and if so, how are they going to be dealt with? Is the franchisor going to retain all of it for its own use or will the franchisor split part of it with the franchisee, or will the franchisor contribute a significant portion, if not all, of the rebate to the advertising fund, for example? It is recommended that rebates be set up as a separate fund.

As a franchisee, this may be the best free advice you will ever get.

The Franchise Agreement is so essential to the success of your relationship with your franchisor that I can only liken it to the foundation of a house. This contract spells out the relationship between the franchisor and the franchisee. The agreement must spell out as clearly as possible the nature of the relationship between the parties, the obligations of the franchisee, the services to be provided by the franchisor, the allocation of the cost of those services between the parties, the fees and other contributions to be paid by the franchisee during the term of the relationship, grounds of termination, effects of termination, treatment of goodwill, and any other restrictions. All oral promises made by each party should be written into the agreement, and the document should be checked clause by clause by a lawyer with a knowledge of franchising.

Consider the following story. A woman decided to buy a franchise with her small inheritance. She had two small children in school and, although her husband was employed, his job was not secure. What she wanted was a second income for the family. But she failed to read and fully understand her contract with the franchisor. It clearly spelled out that the business she was buying had to be open twelve hours a day. With a very small profit margin, it was impossible to hire additional staff, or a babysitter for the children. Her husband finally quit his job to help her in the store. Her primary reason for buying the business was never realized, because she did not pay attention to what was in the contract.

While you may not always read in the contract what you want to see, especially if you have already set your heart on one business in particular, you may be saving yourself considerable heartache and expense down the road if you look carefully before leaping. Keep in mind that dependable, proven franchisors have nothing to hide.

Franchising Your Own Business

Let's examine the advantages and disadvantages of franchising your business. You should not be franchising because you are undercapitalized: it is not a way to solve your financial problems. To franchise, your business will need to be solvent. The quick-buck artist franchisor will be short-lived. Franchising in Canada today has reached a high level of sophistication, even without the legislation to support it. Perhaps because legislation is not in place, franchisees are getting more sophisticated and are better informed. You may consider franchising your business for a variety of good reasons. These are the most common ones: to expand your distribution network without incurring capital expenses; to improve working capital through recovery of costs by selling off locations or rights; to undertake bulk buying in order to take advantage of supplier discounts; to implement selective distribution of products or services; or to merchandise a specialized concept that has recognized consumer acceptance.

One example of the last rationale is Mellanie Stephens's Kettle Creek Canvas Co. The company, in its seventh year, is a manufacturer and marketer of casual, comfortable cotton clothes for men, women, and children. Established in Port Stanley, Ontario, in 1979 while Mellanie was growing vegetables and home-sewing canvas bags, the company projected $10 million in retail sales for 1986.

That success seemed unlikely at the start. The extent of Stephens's manufacturing and retailing experience was limited to sewing canvas bags for her sailboating pals. The bags expanded to a seven-product line, and today there are 100 people who do the sewing for her franchise operation, which spans the country. What started out as "just a little store" has such a reputation that potential franchise holders come looking for her.

Currently, franchise sales are on hold. Says Stephens, "We want to take a look again and make sure we're doing it right. We have not had to go out there and beat the bushes for franchisees. They find us. We've got good franchisees and a good crew of people." Her money originally came from a $15,000 note, cosigned by a friend. She had little business background and she was struggling, but she knew she could grow. "People could identify with my products. They seemed to connect with the look and feel of the store and the product."

Interested investors always ask, "How much money will I make? What happens if you go under? What if I want another store? How much help am I going to get from you?" Good questions. Everything is spelled out in her agreement. If chosen, you can be sure of one thing: she knows people. "You can train all you want, but if there is one particular trait that is most important, it's attitude." Future plans include further expansion into the United States. Canadian operations include manufacturing, retail, and wholesale to five corporate offices and forty-eight franchisees.

Sylvia Nimetz of Winnipeg bought a franchise from Stephens's company with her winnings from SuperLoto. "I was familiar with a Kettle Creek store in Sarnia, liked the concept and clothes, so I took the plunge. But first I spoke with an accountant, a lawyer who was an expert in franchise agreements, government people, then took myself to the library and read books on how to make a bank proposal," says Nimetz. Her advice? "Get good advice from professionals."

As a franchisor, the need for expansive and expensive bureaucratic head offices is often avoided, since franchising is generally administered by a small central organization, with a few highly skilled experts in specific areas of business. One of the hallmarks of a good franchise operation is the extensive delegation of operational details to motivated people. The Toronto-based franchise, Colours, is a company based on colour analysis owned by Brigette Manning, and is considered one of the ten hottest franchise operations in Canada, according to *Canadian Business*. It is one example of minimal staffing. This consulting service, which offers personalized fashion and makeup advice based on colour suitability, produces $15 million in franchise sales, plus another $4.5 million in related head-office revenue, according to Manning. Considering the dollar volume, with over a hundred franchises now world-wide, a traditional corporate setting involving fifty to one hundred employees would not be unusual. Colours has a head-office staff of twenty-five.

As a franchisor you hold more cards in your hand to compete for high discounts or savings in the areas of purchasing, advertising, site availability, and lease negotiations, as well as the distinct advantage of being smiled upon by the banking community. According to banker Al Droppo, "The franchising industry is now sufficiently mature to provide reliable data which clearly confirms that the success ratio of franchise entrepreneurs is much higher than in those start-up cases where franchising is not involved." Another plus for you is that you are able to acquire local expertise. Your franchisees will generally be familiar with their locales, opening up new areas of in-depth information for you. Having this kind of information will give you valuable insight for further expansion. Once the first franchisee has established confidence in that area or territory, further expansion becomes easier. Stability cannot be overlooked. The franchisee will be building a solid business foundation for herself, and, at the same time, implanting your corporate logo or identification in the minds of the populace.

Royalties

Up to now we have considered only the franchise fee as a source of income. Now let's look at royalties. Close to 100 per cent of all franchisors charge their franchisees royalties of between 2 and 9 per cent. Three of the most common methods are: royalties as a percentage of gross sales; as a percentage of cost or product purchases; and as a dollar value multiplied by the number of product units sold. Lawyer Frank Zaid recommends "that rebates be set up as a separate fund." According to his experience, "The general question is, 'What are you doing with rebates?' There are some franchisors who are saying, 'Yes, we are getting rebates on behalf of the system, but they are not significant in the overall purchases that we make. We feel we are entitled to them because as long as you get fair pricing in terms of supply, we should be getting something for arranging this! Now, there are other franchisors who say, 'Yes, we're getting this because of the combined purchasing power of all our franchisees, so why don't we split it on a 50/50 basis.' Then others say, 'We don't want to get involved in any accusations of being unfair, so we'll take all the rebates we can arrange and contribute it the best way we know how, to the benefit of all the franchisees, and put it into the advertising fund.' "

Fixing the rate requires guidance. You must be aware of royalty rates charged by competitors. At the beginning, some franchisors will offer a lower royalty rate to ensure the franchisee a better chance of success. You will need to decide if the royalty rate charged to your franchisee, in addition to other revenues (e.g., product sales), will be enough to cover the costs of maintaining a franchise operation. Keep in mind that you will be incurring more expenses because of support staff, more extensive travel, long-distance communication costs, new product/service development and testing, and corporate advertising, to mention a few.

It should now be clear that a get-rich-quick scheme may not be worth the effort. The investment, as well as organizational back-up for such a venture, is considerable. Which is why, at the beginning, I cautioned that franchising your business is not an alternative to solving your financial problems.

Doreen Braverman, with the retail and manufacturing business The Flag Shop Inc., is currently franchising her operation. With one franchise sold, she is revamping her whole concept. Says Braverman, "I hired a consultant, but he was a disaster. He personally bought into the first franchise, and is now complaining that the concept will not work." Don't be deceived; Braverman's no *ingénue*. With twelve years of success behind The Flag Shop, which produces a $1.8 million plus revenue annually, and a master's degree in business, she still made mistakes. She'll get it ironed out. The bank will provide financing and the rest of the country will get to share in her mission, "to have a Flag Shop in every major centre in the world." Her advice? "Never sell to a group. Don't go into kiosks or malls. Stick with your well-thought-out plan."

Chapter 10

WHERE TO GO FOR HELP

A variety of assistance programs and services are available throughout the country. A surprising amount of information is free. While not all of the agencies listed will meet your needs, use this guide as a source for counselling, publications, feedback, and general assistance. Start with these:

- Your provincial ministry dedicated to small business
- Canadian Business Centre in Ottawa — Zenith 3200 (toll free)
- Statistics Canada in Ottawa (112-800-663-1551) and in major Canadian cities
- Chambers of Commerce and Boards of Trade
- Federal Regional Economic Development Commissions
- The Consumer and Corporate Affairs ministry in Ottawa
- Community colleges
- Your nearest university
- Major financial institutions
- Your local library
- Small-business seminars and lectures

If you have an invention or are creating something you feel is unique, write to Consumer and Corporate Affairs in Ottawa for information on trademarks, patents, industrial designs, and copyright.

National Organizations

The following organizations serve the entire country. The list was compiled by the *Globe and Mail* and appeared in "The Report on Business" on May 29, 1986.

Canadian Organization of Small Business
Suite 310, 7050 Woodbine Avenue
Markham, Ontario L3R 4G8
A non-profit organization supporting and promoting the interest of small business and independent professionals.

The Entrepreneurship Institute of Canada
256 Columbia Street West
Waterloo, Ontario N2L 3L3
A non-profit organization sponsored by major corporations and other organizations to assist and encourage entrepreneurs.

Small Business Secretariat
Department of Regional Industrial Expansion
235 Queen Street
Ottawa, Ontario K1A 0H5
Offers publications on small business as well as maintaining telephone service to offer advice, guidance, and information on federal and corporate programs and services. Offices located in each of the provinces and the two territories.

Federal Business Development Bank
More than eighty offices across the country. A Crown corporation assisting and promoting most types of businesses in Canada at various stages of development. Offers three principal services: financial (loans, loan guarantees, and financial planning), investment banking, and management services (counselling, information, seminars).

Sources of Funds Index
8 Pailton Crescent
Toronto, Ontario M4S 2H8
Publishes directory of more than 500 sources of funds available to businesses in Canada. Listings include government assistance programs and venture capital sources (includes frequent updates).

Canadian Federation of Independent Business
Suite 401, 4141 Yonge Street
Willowdale, Ontario M2P 2A6
Non-profit political-action organization fostered by medium-sized and small businesses throughout the country. It offers education and information services, newsletters, and studies. Keeps members abreast of current social, political, and economic issues affecting owner-operated businesses. Branches in Vancouver, Edmonton, Regina, Quebec City, Winnipeg, and Halifax.

TIEM Canada Inc.
Offices in Mississauga, St. John's, Sydney, Winnipeg, and Vancouver.
Private-sector initiative providing professional support systems for small-business entrepreneurship. Provides training and advisory services during start-up phases. Geared to market assessment,

management skills and training, facilities and support services, employee training, access to seed capital, community support.

Provincial Agencies
Below is an alphabetical listing by province, also taken from the *Globe and Mail* article.

ALBERTA
Ministry of Tourism and Small Business
10025 Jasper Avenue
Edmonton, Alberta T5J 3Z3
Provides counselling assistance for small businesses through ten offices throughout the province. The Alberta Opportunity Co. helps turn ideas into success by lending funds to business people for whom conventional financing is unavailable. It has a head office in Edmonton, plus regional divisions. The market Development Assistance Program provides assistance to Alberta businesses by sharing the financial risks of entering new markets for exporting goods and services. The Canada/Alberta Tourism Agreement encourages new private-sector investment in the province's tourist industry through incentives. The Alberta Wage Subsidy Program assists businesses in the creation of new jobs. *Starting a Business in Alberta* is a handbook providing information on starting a business in the province.

BRITISH COLUMBIA
Ministry of Industry and Small Business Development
1045 Douglas Street
Victoria, B.C. V8W 3C1
Provides counselling assistance for small business through forty offices throughout the province, serviced on a rotating basis. Provides numerous pamphlets and booklets free of charge. There is a Small Business Incentives Agreement for small and medium-sized business. Includes Small Manufacturers' Incentive Program and Agriculture Incentive Program. Industrial Diversification Program provides contributions up to a maximum of 30 per cent of eligible capital costs and for loans up to a maximum of 50 per cent of eligible capital costs. Resource Industries Value-Added Program provides low-interest loans up to a maximum of 50 per

cent of eligible capital costs. Business Development Program provides management assistance, management development, assistance to associations, and student venture loans. Discovery Enterprises Inc., a venture capital fund, is financed through the province and designed to encourage advanced technology. B.C. Innovation Office assists companies and individuals to acquire expertise and money for the development, production, and sale of new products and processes. Contact also the Discovery Foundation, Suite 200, Discovery Park, 3700 Gilmore Way, Burnaby, B.C. V5G 4M1.

MANITOBA
Manitoba Business Development and Tourism
155 Carlton Street
Winnipeg, Manitoba R3C 3H8
Department plays dual role: Small Business and Regional Development, and Travel Manitoba. Has comprehensive counselling service to small-business community, stimulates entrepreneurship, fosters new business, aids existing business in expansion, and teaches management techniques. Business Development Centres in Winnipeg, Brandon, and Dauphin offer seminars in management skills for emerging entrepreneurs and courses for established small-business operators. Other projects include Venture Capital Program, Feasibility Assistance for Small Manufacturers, Design Assistance for Small Projects, and Commercial Planning and Development Program.

NEW BRUNSWICK
Department of Commerce and Development
Small Business Division
P.O. Box 6000
Fredericton, New Brunswick E3B 5H1
Administers Small Industry Financial Assistance Program in conjunction with twelve regional economic development commissions.

NEWFOUNDLAND AND LABRADOR
Department of Development and Tourism
P.O. Box 4750
St. John's, Newfoundland A1C 5T7
Ocean Industry Development programs include market and product development, applied research and development, establishment and

expansion, marketing/product enhancement, business and community development, and opportunities identification/project enhancement. The Tourism branch provides incentives program for tourism. Newfoundland and Labrador Development Corporation assists small- and medium-sized businesses to locate in the province, and modernize and/or expand operations in manufacturing, processing, tourism, and offshore-related services.

NOVA SCOTIA
Department of Development
World Trade and Convention Centre
1800 Argyle Street
P.O. Box 519
Halifax, Nova Scotia B3J 2R7
Has eleven regional branches. Oceans Industries Innovation Centre provides help to small businesses in establishing or expanding innovative directions relating to oceans industries. Small Business Secretariat assists small- or medium-sized businesses by providing general information and help with problems relating to government regulations.

ONTARIO
Ministry of Industry, Trade and Technology
Small Business Branch
900 Bay Street
Toronto, Ontario M7A 2E4
Ministry has eighteen regional offices. Offers a variety of coordinated programs to assist Ontario industries and businesses in specific ventures. Export Success Fund helps exporters by covering some costs of exporting products manufactured in province. Small Business Development Corporation provides incentives to individuals, corporations, and other prescribed organizations investing in the corporation, which directs funds and provides business and managerial expertise to eligible small businesses. Ministry of Tourism and Recreation encourages economic development and employment growth by providing selective financial assistance for the establishment of new tourism facilities, as well as expansion, renovation, and winterization of existing establishments located in areas where tourism is of major importance to the economy.

PRINCE EDWARD ISLAND
Department of Industry
Industrial Development Division
P.O. Box 2000
Charlottetown, Prince Edward Island C1A 7N8
Small Business Incentive Program loans for modernization, expansion, or creation of new operation. The PEI Lending Authority provides capital loans and operating credit for small business, tourist operators, farmers, and fishermen. Rural Business Centre Program provides financial assistance to selected communities to help create suitable new commercial space as well as encourage new entrepreneurs. Cultural Product Development Fund designed to stimulate development of PEI cultural products.

QUEBEC
Industrial Development Corporation
Suite 700, 1125 Chemin Saint-Louis
Sillery, Quebec G1S 1E5
Government office with six regional offices assisting economic development by granting financial incentives. Business Assistance Program promotes new job opportunities for tourist, manufacturing, and service industries. Assistance Program for the Development of Tourism provides incentives for the promotion of tourism and/or tourism industry. Investment Assistance Program for Manufacturing Companies provides grants in support of Quebec manufacturers involved in significant technological or innovative manufacturing.

SASKATCHEWAN
Department of Tourism and Small Business
Bank of Montreal Building
2103 11th Avenue
Regina, Saskatchewan S4P 3V7
Business Resource Centres are located in seven areas of the province, with storefront centres providing information and advisory services for new businesses. Canada-Saskatchewan Tourist Agreement provides assistance available for wide range of tourism projects. Northern Saskatchewan Revolving Fund is a program for business ventures in northern Saskatchewan which are owned and

operated by northern residents. Management Assistance Program offers five-month program coordinated by the department, local Chambers of Commerce, and other business and trade organizations to improve business operations. Youth Entrepreneur Program provides financial assistance to Saskatchewan youth starting new permanent ventures in the province.

TERRITORIES
Northwest Territories Department of
Economic Development and Tourism
Box 1320
Yellowknife, Northwest Territories X1A 2L9
Through loan and guarantee funds the department offers assistance to new businesses or those wishing to expand.

Yukon Department of Economic Development
Mines and Small Business
Box 2703
Whitehorse, Yukon Y1A 2C6
Business Loan Fund provides capital for new businesses or for expansion. Renewable Resource Economic Development Unit for innovators launching a business using renewable resources. Trade Show Assistance Program provides travel assistance to business people to expand Yukon markets.

Most provinces have some form of Student Venture Capital Program, as well as a department dedicated to women, some exclusively to women in business. Make use of government as well as private-sector sources of information. And while you are asking questions, find out about any associations such as Association of Women Business Owners, Women in Business, Women's Networking, or any other association founded with women in mind.

Glossary

Some of the definitions below are adapted from *A Dictionary of Canadian Economics* (Edmonton: Hurtig, 1980), which should be consulted for further reference.

Accountant Someone who carries out the bookkeeping, auditing, and other financial reporting and analysis of the company.
Accounts payable Outstanding bills of the firm; money owed to suppliers for goods and services purchased for the normal operation of the business.
Accounts receivable Monies owed to the company by customers for goods or services purchased from it.
Assets The entire accumulated property of a person or company that can be used to pay debts or expenses, including cash on hand and money owed by customers. Assets are those things that a business owns. *See* **Current assets, Fixed assets,** and **Liquid assets.**
Audit An annual financial examination of a business, conducted by an independent firm of accountants whose study is acceptable to Revenue Canada, your bank, and your shareholders.
Balance sheet A written statement showing what a business owns and what it owes at a given point in time. The difference between its property (including cash) and its debts is shown as its net worth, which is usually divided among the shareholders.
Bad debts Money owed to a business by customers who cannot pay.
Break-even point The level of sales (or production) required for a company to show neither a profit nor a loss.
Capital The total funds invested in a company to enable it to carry on its business.
Cashflow The amount of money left in a specific period of time after all cash income is accounted for and all cash expenses are paid. If expenses are greater than cash income, then you have a

negative cashflow and require additional sources of funding.

Cash poor While a business may be profitable, it may have little cash on hand because of rapid expansion, for example, so the enterprise cannot be supported by profits alone. Such a business is currently cash poor.

Co-op Three or more people who contribute their time, product or service to an organization for sale by that organization, which deducts the cost of sales and distribution from its total income and distributes the remainder to co-op members on an equal or pro-rata basis, based on contribution.

Cost of sales (or Cost of goods sold) The direct costs of acquiring and/or producing an item for sale or of providing a service, exclusive of overhead.

Current assets Cash, and property that will be sold or converted to cash within one year.

Current liabilities Debts that will be paid within one year.

Depreciation The costs to a firm for fixed assets (machinery, buildings, equipment) that wear out or lose value over a period of time in the normal operation of the business. Depreciation costs are tax-deductible.

Disbursements Money paid out by a company to its suppliers and other creditors to cover operating expenses.

Equity The property and income of a firm after all creditors have been paid off. **Equity capital** is the money in the firm that represents ownership, expressed usually in common shares owned by investors.

Financial statements Charts and/or schedules that reflect some aspect of the financial situation of the company.

Fixed assets Usually real property or depreciable materials. Through buying or selling them you can increase or decrease the company's worth.

Fixed costs Business expenses that do not vary with the volume of business.

Fixed expenses Predictable and firm expenses that are ongoing over a long period of time, such as rent, utilities, rental equipment, and salaries.

Forecasting Predicting how many units will be sold in a given time frame, at what cost to you, and at what price to the end user, in order to quantify the manufacturing needs, economic support, and human resources necessary for success.

Gross profit The sales income of a business before expenses, depreciation, and taxes are deducted.

Income The total cash coming to the business from a variety of sources, such as customer payments, interest, tax credits, dividends, and bonuses.

Income and expense statement A monthly or quarterly report detailing the source and amount of all income and the total costs (sales, wages, benefits) of a business, broken down into sub-headings, that can be compared month to month, season to season, or year to year.

Inventory Manufactured but unsold stock, on-hand and available for sale immediately.

Invested share capital The money that shareholders and lenders put up initially to start the company.

Investors Persons or corporations investing money for future benefit, profit or income.

Leasehold improvements Physical alterations inside a leased building to create office, manufacturing or warehouse space along with reception, customer and administration functions.

Liabilities Immediate and future financial obligations that expand and contract with the sales success of a product or service. *See* **Current liabilities** and **Long-term liabilities.**

Liquid assets Cash, and property that can quickly and easily be sold for cash.

Liquidity The speed and ease with which property can be converted into cash at market value, assuming that there are willing buyers.

Long-term liabilities Debts that will not be paid off within one year.

Losses The amount of money by which expenses exceed income.

Management structure The hierarchy of people and their relationship to each other as well as to the corporation or business. Can be called the **Management team**.

Market The potential buyers of a product or service, determined by such factors as geographic, economic, and social characteristics. The demand for something (product or service), including the price at which it will sell well. The market is expressed in types and numbers of consumers.

Market analysis The process of determining the characteristics of the potential consumers of your product or service as well as the size of the group and the depth of penetration you might hope to achieve, when considering costs and competition.
Marketing Any plan that describes a strategy for making your potential customers aware of your goods and services and to purchasing them. It includes promotion, publicity, advertising, and sales.
Net profit Income left after expenses, depreciation, and taxes are deducted.
Operating costs Expenses incurred in conducting the ordinary and necessary activities of a business.
Partnership A legal association of two or more persons in a business enterprise. Partners share the workload, risks, profits, and losses of the business, depending on the partnership agreement.
Profit The financial gain from an undertaking. *See* **Gross profit** and **Net profit.**
Profit-and-loss statement A breakdown of income and expenses, showing the profit or loss for a certain period of time.
Proprietary interest A patent, pending or accepted, usually in Canada, the United States, or the United Kingdom for a period of seven years. It disallows any other corporation in the world from duplicating the invention without paying a royalty fee.
Real property The land occupied by a building, as well as the building itself, that serves as the location of your business.
Revenue The total income a business firm receives from all sources.
Sales forecast A prediction of the number of units you will sell within a specified period of time and at a given price.
Shareholder's equity The amount by which the value of a company's property exceeds that of its debts, divided by the number of shares. When debts exceed property (including cash), the shareholder is then said to be in a negative equity position.
Spin-off The establishment of a new corporation for the management of a product or service taken away from the original organization.
Start-up The beginning of an operation, venture, business or service; the developmental stage, prior to receipt of income.
Start-up capital The total amount of money, resources, and property that a company or a person requires to begin the operation

of a business and sustain it until income is received.
Statement of income A summary report of all forms of income available — sales, gratuities, tax credits, dividends, and receivables.
Target market A very specific group of potential customers defined by age, lifestyle, sex, socio-economic position, income, geography, needs, and interests.
Tax credit Monies owing from government as a result of a change in legislation, overpayment, business losses, or a change in one's personal situation. The credit is usually averaged over a number of years.
Variable costs Expenses that vary with the volume of business.
Venture A new undertaking created on speculation to make money, especially one in which there is a considerable degree of risk or uncertainty.
Venture capital The money that a company or person invests in a new business undertaking.
Working capital The difference between current property and current debts; or that current property (including money) not financed by current debts.

BIBLIOGRAPHY

Aarsteinsen, Barbara. "Unparalleled Growth is Predicted." *Globe and Mail*. 24 July, 1986.

Annett, William. "Managing Cash." *B.C. Business*. January, 1986.

British Columbia, Ministry of Small Business Development. *Independent Business Handbook*. Victoria, 1984.

British Columbia Innovation Office. *New Venture Business Planning*. Vancouver, n.d.

Bruneau, Claude and Barbara Allen. "Financial Know-How: Women Tap Into a Potent Power Source." *Business Quarterly*, Vol. 49, No. 1 (1984).

Carson, Susan. "Female Entrepreneurs Told They Have More." Montreal *Gazette*. 31 March, 1986.

Crane, David. *A Dictionary of Canadian Economics*. Edmonton: Hurtig, 1980.

Crawford, Michael. "Look Before You Leap." *Small Business*. August, 1986.

Federal Business Development Bank. *Buying a Franchise*. Minding Your Own Business Series No. 20. 1979.

Federal Business Development Bank. *Legal Structures of a Small Business: Management Clinic Workbook No. 4*. Montreal, 1981.

Forrest, Diane. "Part-time Sales: A Beginner's Guide." *Chatelaine*. October 1985.

Foster, Cecil. "Entrepreneurs Set to Fly High." *Globe and Mail*, 24 July, 1986.

Freudenberger, Dr. Herbert J. and Gail North. *Women's Burn-out*. Garden City: Doubleday, 1985.

Gawain, Shatki. *Creative Visualization*. New York: Bantam, 1978.

Gélinas, Guy-André. ''The Role and Services of the Federal Government in Franchising.'' Canada: Department of Industry, Trade and Commerce, 1980.

Gibbons, Maurice and Gary Phillips. *Self Education as a Deliberate Lifestyle: An Introduction to the Skills of Self-Directed Learning*. Vancouver: Simon Fraser University, Challenge Education Project, IDEA., 1981. Unpublished.

Gray, Douglas A. *The Entrepreneur's Self-Assessment Guide*. Vancouver: International Self-Counsel Press, 1986.

Henderson, Rachelle. ''Lise Watier Is Taking On the World.'' Montreal *Gazette*. 16 June, 1986.

Hennig, Margaret, and Anne Jardim. *The Managerial Woman*. New York: Pocket Books, 1976.

Hossie, Linda. ''National Research Undermined: Women Inventors Face Problems.'' *Globe and Mail*. 6 March, 1986.

Jacks, Evelyn. ''Tax and the Small Business Owner.'' *Canadian Consumer*. Vol. 16, No. 1. (January, 1986).

Jennings, William E. *Entrepreneurship: A Primer for Canadians*. Toronto: Canadian Foundation for Economic Education, 1985.

Jensen, Knud. *Canadian Business*. September, 1985.

Johnson, Bob. ''Tip-Sheet For Tomorrow.'' *Small Business*. January/February, 1986.

Katz, Robert. ''A Guide for Forming Partnerships.'' *B.C. Industry and Small Business News*. Victoria: B.C. Ministry of Industry and Small Business Development. June 1982. Vol. 3, No. 3.

Kentridge, Catherine. ''I Figured I Had The Smarts To Do Anything I Wanted.'' *Small Business*. November, 1984. Vol. 3, No. 9.

Kentridge, Catherine. ''Montreal's Blooming.'' *Small Business*. July/August, 1985.

Kolbenschlag, Madonna. *Kiss Sleeping Beauty Good-Bye*. Garden City: Doubleday, 1979.

Lakein, Alan. *How to Get Control of Your Time and Your Life*. New York: New American Library, 1973.

Litton, Moneca. ''The Relationship of Female Entrepreneurship With Lending Institutions in Western Canada — Perceptions Versus Realities.'' Unpublished report written for Royal Bank of Canada. May, 1985.

Mitchell, Meg. ''A Profile of the Canadian Woman Director.'' *Business Quarterly*. Vol. 49, No. 1 (1984).

Naisbitt, John. ''Naisbitt Predicts Bright Future.'' *The Franchise Handbook*. No. 3. (1986).

Pipa, Alison. ''Franchising Could Be Route to Becoming Your Own Boss.'' *Globe and Mail*. 24 July, 1986.

Robinson, Marie. ''Here's Help in Shopping for an Accountant.'' *Small Business*. December, 1985.

Salter, Michael. ''The 'New' Businesswoman.'' *The Financial Times*, 4 August, 1984.

Scollard, Jeanette R. *The Self-Employed Woman*. New York: Simon and Schuster, 1985.

Secretan, Lance. *Managerial Moxie*. New York: Holt, Rinehart & Winston, (1986).

Spicer, Keith. ''Today's Ambitious Woman Starts Own Business.'' Vancouver *Province*. 15 August, 1986.

Stevenson, Lois. ''An Investigation of the Entrepreneurial Experience of Women: Implications for Small Business Policy in Canada.'' Wolfville: Fred C. Manning School of Business, Acadia University, 1984.

Templeman-Kluit, Anne. ''I'll Start My Own Darn School.'' *Atlantic Insight*. May, 1986.

Von Dech, Roger, *A Whack on the Side of the Head*. New York: Warner Books, 1983.

Walker, Kathleen. ''Baby Boomers Hit the Big One.'' Vancouver *Sun*. 12 July 1986.

White, Jerry, ''The Rise of Female Capitalism — Women as Entrepreneurs.'' *Business Quarterly*. Vol. 49, No. 1 (1984).

Winston, Sandra. *The Entrepreneurial Woman*. New York: Newsweek Books, 1979.

Wyatt, Elaine. ''Women a Growing Force in Small Business.'' *Financial Times*. 22 July 1985.

INDEX